This book is dedicated to all the fine saxophonists
and composers whom I have omitted to mention

YEHUDI MENUHIN MUSIC GUIDES

Saxophone

Paul Harvey

KAHN & AVERILL, LONDON

First published in 1995 by
Kahn & Averill
9 Harrington Road, London, SW7 3ES

Reprinted in 1997

Reprinted (updated) in 2002

British Library Cataloguing in Publication Data

A catalogue record for this book is available from the British Library

ISBN 1-871082-53-6

Typeset in Times by YHT Ltd., London
Printed in Great Britain by
Halstan & Co Ltd., Amersham, Bucks

Contents

List of Illustrations

Acknowledgements

To my daughter, Paulina, for word processing and proof reading;
Fred Summerbell, for invaluable technical advice and
Michael Farnham, my chief photographer.

Also to the following friends and colleagues who have gener-
ously supplied me with information, photographs, instruments
and encouragement.

Dave Aarons, Billy Amstell, David Bilger, Jim Clow, Paul
Cohen, June Emerson, James Gillespie, Christopher Gradwell,
John Harle, Wally Horwood, Theodore McDowell, Henry
Mackenzie, Peter Nichols, James Rae, Peter Ripper, John Rip-
per, John Sands, Frank Slack, Gerald Style, Roger Swift, Neville
Thomas, Stephen Trier, Alfred Wallbank, and His Majesty King
Bhumibol Adulyadej of Thailand.

Introduction

One of the most frequent types of letter I receive is from the young saxophonist doing a project on the instrument, asking me to recommend books as reference sources. I have a standard list which I photocopy and send back, but as I do so, I am aware of its shortcomings.

There are quite a few books about the saxophone in existence, but, of course, not nearly as many as for most other instruments. The main problem, however, is that most of them are published in France or in the U.S.A., and, even if obtainable in this country, they tend to be very expensive. Also, to gain an overall knowledge of the saxophone it would be necessary to read all of them; I can think of no single book which covers all aspects of the instrument; they all tend to concentrate in great detail on one particular subject; history, acoustics, playing or repertoire, etc.

Therefore, my aim in this book is to provide the young project writer with all the necessary information under one cover, at the same time indicating where a more detailed and specialised study of any one aspect of the instrument may be continued.

Having sometimes been asked to mark or assess such finished projects, I have often noticed that the writer has suffered from an excess of information on one particular subject. I recognise the source material, but often the project writer has selected something superfluous to quote, omitting the really vital information, through lack of practical experience.

So in this book, I shall attempt to provide the basic facts which are required to understand the instrument, to play it well, and, eventually, to teach it to others.

One
The Classification of the Saxophone

The first necessity in a book about the saxophone must be to clarify where it belongs in the families of instruments. As its body is obviously metallic, many people labour under the delusion that the saxophone must be a member of the brass family. Even if the dreaded mis-spelling SAXAPHONE is avoided, one often sees saxophone music included in the 'Music for Brass' section of shops or catalogues.

However, the classification of wind instruments is not quite as straightforward as that; it has nothing to do with the material of which the instruments are made. If it had, then in a modern orchestra the flutes would have to go and sit among the trumpets and trombones, wouldn't they, for when did you last see a wooden flute?

The brass family has only one common denominator; not the use of valves, for then the slide trombone would not qualify; it must be the cup shaped mouthpiece, which is placed against the lips, not between them.

The woodwind family also has only one common denominator, and it's not their being made of wood; beside the now almost exclusively metal flute, there have been metal clarinets, even metal oboes, and the most popular make of contrabass clarinet is metal. It's not the reed; oboes and bassoons have a double reed; clarinets and saxophones a beak shaped mouthpiece and single reed; flutes do not use a reed at all, the player blowing across the top of a tone hole.

So, the woodwind's common denominator must be that the pitch of the notes is altered by opening and closing holes in the body of the instrument, as opposed to the brass family, where

1

the whole length of tube is employed for every note, being altered by the valves which direct the vibrating air column through various different lengths of tubing. On a brass instrument every note comes out through the bell, whereas on a woodwind instrument only the lowest note comes directly out of the bell, all the others partly issuing from one or more of the holes in the instrument's bore. This is why mutes are successful on brass instruments but not on woodwinds.

Materials used in the manufacture of wind instruments are chosen for practical reasons. Wooden trumpets and horns are a possibility, but would be very difficult and expensive to make. Clarinets are frequently made of plastic nowadays, and there was once a popular make of plastic saxophone.

Wooden saxophones, although they would work, would be impractical to manufacture in the larger sizes, but consider the Hungarian folk instrument, the tarogato; this is virtually a wooden soprano saxophone, and it works extremely well, having a rather more mellow sound than a metal soprano saxophone.

The other mistake often made about the saxophone is to refer to it as a 'hybrid' instrument. This is not so; it is a pure woodwind instrument, having a reed, beak mouthpiece, and the pitch altered by means of holes. A hybrid instrument is one where a cup mouthpiece produces a vibrating air column in a tube with holes, such as the cornett, ophicleide or serpent. Hypothetically, an instrument with a reed producing a vibrating air column altered in length by valves would also be a hybrid, if such a thing existed.

So, we see that the saxophone is a complete member of the woodwind family, although it happens to have a metal body.

Choosing An Instrument

Most saxophonists start on the alto, but there is no very important reason why one should not start on another size. All saxophones have the same fingering, but the advantage of starting on the alto comes when you want to play with a piano, as in the past most easy music was written with the piano accompaniment for Eb saxophone. Nowadays, music publishers are recognising the fact that some people want to start on tenor, and are publishing more easy music with B♭ piano accompaniments, but the alto still has a lot more music available.

The only really reliable way to test a saxophone is to play it, so if you are a beginner it is essential to get a teacher before you get an instrument. Either ask the teacher to obtain an instrument for you, or let the first lesson be going to a shop with the teacher to select an instrument.

What model you go for will depend on how much you can afford to spend. Saxophones are like cars; you get what you pay for! It is possible for a beginner to get along quite nicely on a cheap clarinet for a couple of years, provided that the pads cover properly and it has a good mouthpiece. Unfortunately, the saxophone is more like the flute, in that the cheapest instruments are very difficult to play. In the case of the saxophone this is because of the conical bore, which makes the low notes very hard to get unless every pad is airtight.

Nearly all the best makes of saxophone are either French or Japanese, and the leading manufacturers all offer a wide range of student models as well as the most expensive professional models, so go for the best one you can afford. The second-hand market is purely a matter of luck, and you would have to be guided entirely by your teacher. The saxophone has increased in popularity so much over the last few years that there are not as many second-hand instruments available as there once were.

There are a few visual checks you can make:

Are the pads closing firmly and centrally on the holes; is the circular impression of the hole's rim central on the pad?

Does the spring tension close the keys firmly? Better that the springs should be a little too strong than too weak.

Do the black rollers between the little finger keys turn freely?

Feel the rods on which the keys are mounted. Is there any play between their ends and the posts which connect them to the body?

Move each key up and down. You should hear no clicks of metal against metal; corks or felt should cushion each point of contact.

COMPARISON OF BORES
L–R: Hungarian Tarogato (Stowasser of Budapest, Kneller Hall collection)
Modern Selmer B♭ soprano saxophone (author's collection) Metal clarinet (no
name, probably Hawkes & Son; Alfred Wallbank collection) (Note the
cylindrical bore of the clarinet, in comparison to the others, which are all
conical in varying degrees) C soprano saxophone (no name, author's
collection) Oboe (no name, author's collection)

COMPARISON OF BORES
Reverse View

But here is the most important point of all for a beginner: You could buy the most expensive instrument available, but if you try to play it with an unsuitable mouthpiece, you have wasted your money!

When you are an experienced player you can experiment with a wide range of different mouthpieces, but it is essential to learn to play correctly from the start on a mouthpiece with a MEDIUM-CLOSE lay.

The most expensive mouthpieces are unlikely to be the best for a beginner; they are usually metal, more of which are made with wide lays; excellent mouthpieces for certain types of work, but NOT for learning the instrument!

The beginner needs a black mouthpiece (ebonite/hard rubber) with a lay such as, in letters, C or C star, or in numbers, 3 or 4. It's impossible to be more specific, as all makers use a different system of grading for their mouthpieces, but remember, it's MEDIUM-CLOSE to start on.

Two
The History of the Saxophone

Most woodwind instruments have evolved over a long period, often from a folk instrument, which has gradually been refined for concert use, having its tuning improved and extra keywork added bit by bit. No one person can be said to have 'invented' the flute, oboe or bassoon. The clarinet is usually credited to Johann Christoph Denner of Nuremberg, who added a speaker key to the ancient chalumeau in about 1700, giving it a second register overblowing at the twelfth. The clarinet as we know it today dates from 1839, when Klosé applied the ring-key system, developed for the flute by Theobald Boehm, to the clarinet, hence the name which still survives; the Boehm system.

The saxophone, however, is unique in that it was the invention of one man, whose name it bears: Adolphe Sax. He was born in Dinant, Belgium, on November 6th, 1814, and christened Antoine Joseph Sax, although known as Adolphe throughout his life.

His father was the instrument maker, Charles Joseph Sax (1793–1865), who moved to Brussels with his family soon after Adolphe was born. It was here, in the Belgian capital, that the young Adolphe watched his father doing his important work to develop a chromatic horn, later assisting him in all the varied engineering skills necessary to make woodwind and brass instruments.

At the same time Adolphe was receiving a musical education, studying first the flute, and, later, the clarinet with Valentine Bender, Bandmaster of the Royal Guides (The Belgian equivalent of the French Garde Républicaine Band). It is well documented that he became a very good player; the German

7

Adolphe Sax

composer, Küffner, dedicated a clarinet duet to the twenty year old Sax. But he had already been making instruments and displaying them at exhibitions from the age of sixteen, and this became his main preoccupation.

At first, during the 1830's, he mostly worked on improvements to the clarinet, but soon he became interested in what had, until then, been the almost insuperable problem of manufacturing a viable bass clarinet, an octave below the normal B flat instrument. He produced his first model in 1838, which immediately proved to be superior to all previous bass clarinets, and Sax was soon in great demand to play his new instrument.

The design and production of the first really successful bass clarinet was Sax's greatest contribution to the Symphony Orchestra as we know it today.

Concurrent with this he commenced his great work on the brass family; the invention of a whole new range of conical bore brass instruments with valves, later known as 'saxhorns', which, to this day, are the basis of the Brass Band.

The turning point in Adolphe Sax's career came in 1841, when, for two main reasons, he decided to move to Paris. The first was the decision of the Brussels Exhibition jury that year; although Sax's display of instruments was much admired, they pronounced him too young to receive the first prize. While he was still in a state of acute frustration at this ruling, he received a visit from Lieutenant Général Comte de Rumigny, of the French Army. The gist of his message was this: The General had heard of Sax's precocious talent as a designer and maker of wind instruments, and his interest persuaded Sax to make the move to Paris.

He is reputed to have arrived in the French capital with only thirty francs to his name; rather inadequate funds to set up a musical instrument factory! Nevertheless, this is exactly what he achieved in a remarkably short time, thanks to loans arranged by several influential friends, including the composer, Hector Berlioz, who was to remain Sax's most notable champion.

The first Parisian workshop of Adolphe Sax was set up at No. 10, rue Saint-Georges, in the ninth arrondissement. It was here that the saxophone was first constructed, during the five years from 1841 until the original patent was taken out on March 21st, 1846.

Although this is the official date when the saxophone is usually said to have come into existence, Sax had been experimenting with the idea of a single reed and beak mouthpiece, vibrating an air column in a conical metal tube with holes and keys, for several years before that. One of the instruments which his father made quite frequently was the ophicleide; bass of the keyed bugle family; a hybrid instrument with a cup mouthpiece, conical bore, holes and keys. There must usually have been one of these lying about in the Brussels workshop during the period when Adolphe was working on the bass clarinet, and he almost certainly must have tried the experiment of replacing the ophicleide's cup mouthpiece with a bass clarinet mouthpiece and reed.

This has often been done in modern times, and the result persuasively demonstrates the probable derivation of the saxophone. Even more so because Sax first thought of the instrument as a bass voice, the first working saxophone he made being of that size. Another reason for this may have been that this was the register in which the woodwind sections of French Army Bands needed strengthening. However, he immediately realised its potential as a whole family of instruments, as the 1846 patent mentions no less than eight different sizes!

All this was accomplished in spite of an incredibly vicious campaign by the established Parisian instrument makers, who resented the technical brilliance of the young Belgian newcomer, who, admittedly, did nothing to ingratiate himself with his competitors, and was outspoken in his criticism of existing instruments.

The culmination of this vendetta was an attempt on Sax's life in 1845, in which one of his employees was mistaken, in the dark, for Sax himself, and was stabbed to death.

The saxophone first appeared in public two years before the patent was taken out. Berlioz arranged a concert at the Salle Herz on February 3rd 1844, featuring a sextet of Sax's instruments; three brass and three woodwind, Adolphe himself playing the bass part on the newly constructed saxophone. Berlioz had arranged his *Chant Sacré*, an early choral work, to show off the instruments, each playing an extended cadenza in turn. Legend has it that the saxophone cadenza started with a left hand note, which Sax held for an inordinately long time, while he made mechanical adjustments to the keywork with his right hand.

It does seem to be true that he barely finished putting the instrument together in time for the concert, and the audience was growing restive by the time the sextet eventually came onto the platform. The one-handed running repairs may be apocryphal, but it makes a good story!

In 1847 a saxophone class was established at the Gymnase de Musique Militaire (a sort of 19th century French Kneller Hall) and some Regimental Bands began to use saxophones.

Sax had his premises at rue Saint-Georges enlarged to the dimensions of a proper factory, which included a concert hall where he put on concerts to demonstrate his instruments.

Only a decade after the saxophone's debut, it was beginning to spread around the world. The following newspaper cutting, referring to its first appearance in Australia, does not, unfortunately, mention the name of the soloist. It was, however, almost certainly Souallé, who was saxophone soloist with Jullien's Orchestra, introducing the instrument into England for the first time in 1850. It is known that Souallé later toured India, the Far East and Australia, often featuring his own compositions, *Souvenirs of Java* and *Souvenirs of Shanghai*.

The Melbourne Argus – June 11th 1853

Amongst the flood of talent of various sorts which is setting in upon our shores, a foreign gentleman has lately arrived who performs with very considerable skill upon a newly-invented and most remarkable instrument styled the saxophone. This instrument is a sort of combination of the clarionet and the ophicleide, if our readers can understand such an union. The sound is produced by a reed, as in the manner of the clarionet but the body of the instrument being metallic, of large size, and very elaborately keyed, a power is given to it of a most startling kind; a very astonishing compass; and a certain solidity combined with sweetness which is calculated to make the saxophone a very valuable

11

addition to the orchestra, as well as a pleasing instrument for solo performances. Its first introduction is to take place at a grand concert on Monday evening at the Mechanics, the preparations for which are on a very extensive scale. The orchestra is, we believe, to be as well attended as on the evening of the concert given by Herr Strebinger, of which we had to speak so highly; and if the performance is equal to that, it will be very well worth hearing, as no such music was ever before heard in this colony.

In 1857, Sax was appointed Professor of Saxophone at the Paris Conservatoire. This set the seal on the acceptance of the instrument by the musical establishment. At the same time he started his own music publishing company, commissioning many saxophone pieces for his concerts at rue Saint-Georges and test pieces for the Conservatoire. These were written by his many composer friends, such as Singelée, Demersseman, Savari and Arban, the celebrated cornet virtuoso, who was Sax's principal demonstrator of brass instruments.

During the 1850's and 1860's the saxophone became well established as a military band instrument, even gaining acceptance in England, where the Royal Artillery Band used two altos and two tenors as early as the mid 1850's. Life was never easy for Sax himself during this period, however, as his competitors continued to hound him ceaselessly with extremely involved lawsuits, challenging his various patents.

In 1870, the Franco-Prussian War brought disaster on many fronts. From the saxophone's point of view, the worst result was the closure of the class at the Conservatoire, not to be resumed until the appointment of Marcel Mule in 1942! This inexplicable gap of seventy-two years in the serious teaching of the instrument prevented many composers of that period, who would otherwise have written effectively for it, from realising its potential.

Sax's financial affairs deteriorated to the point where he went bankrupt in 1873. The rue Saint-Georges factory was closed and his instrument stock sold in 1877. His sons kept the name of Sax going as a smaller instrument company at No. 84, rue Myrha until 1914. Adolphe Sax himself died at the age of eighty on February 4th, 1894.

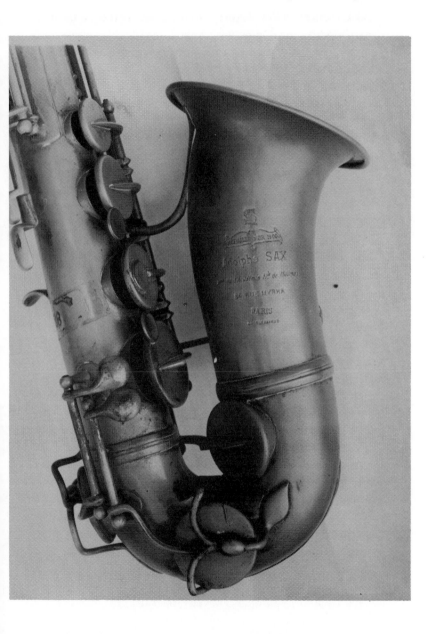

The bell of a 1900 alto saxophone showing the address of Adolphe Sax's
sons' workshop: 84 rue Myrha (Kneller Hall collection)

13

From the turn of the century it could be said that the epicentre of saxophone development travelled Westwards across the Atlantic. Not that the saxophone was a new arrival in the USA; it had been there for nearly fifty years. One Harvey Dodworth, Bandmaster of the 13th Regiment, is said to have first introduced the saxophone into the USA, but it was mainly Eduard Lefèbre who brought the instrument to the notice of the American public. He came over from France with Antoine Jullien's Orchestra in 1853, staying to become an American citizen in 1884, having been a member of Patrick Gilmore's band (the 22nd Regiment of New York) from 1873.

Gilmore died in 1892, and Lefèbre joined the Sousa Band. He formed a Saxophone Quartet in 1905 which toured extensively until his death in 1911, at the age of seventy-seven.

The saxophone continued to thrive as a band instrument, and this was the heyday of popular wind bands in America. But the next significant stage in the saxophone's stylistic odyssey was heralded by a man born in Detroit in 1893; the legendary Rudy Wiedoeft. In his short life of forty-six years he became the most prolific composer-performer the saxophone has ever known. He was a kind of bridge into the jazz age; certainly not a jazz player himself; rather a technical master of the instrument, influenced by 'ragtime' and devoting his talents to short, tuneful, flashy, light 'novelty' numbers, which were immensely popular with the public.

Wiedoeft's work was the apex of the incredible saxophone craze which exploded at the end of the first World War and continued through the 1920's, to some extent pre-dating the saxophone's emergence as an important jazz voice. Many people nowadays, who equate the saxophone with jazz, may find it difficult to believe that, at first, the instrument met with almost as much opposition in that field as in the Symphonic world. The New Orleans purists, with their beloved front line 'Holy Trinity' of cornet, clarinet and trombone, considered the saxophone a commercialised, interloping 'novelty' instrument!

For the first time in this historical account, I can introduce a personal experience. Believe it or not, as late as 1948, when I was a thirteen year old clarinettist in a Trad Band in Sheffield, considering myself a big wheel in the great British post-war trad revival, I can remember voicing anti-saxophone sentiments! Of course, it was just a pseudo-purist pose, typical of a teenager, but I considered myself at one with Bunk Johnson and King Oliver, whose similar opinions I had read or heard somewhere. Don't worry, I soon recovered! Not so the jazz historian, Rex Harris. In his book *Jazz*, published by Pelican Books in 1952, he wrote:

> The tenor-saxophonist, Coleman Hawkins, possessed great powers of improvisation which, had they been canalized into a different medium of expression, e.g. the clarinet, might well have secured him a permanent place in jazz.

It is strange to reflect that this amazing statement was made at a time when, in New York, Charlie Parker was at the height of his powers, and The Hawk himself was to have a further 17 years of prolific jazz life!

Back in the real world of 1920's America, the centre of jazz development moved north to Chicago, where the public wanted to hear saxophones, so that is where the jazz saxophone section really started. Before very long the two altos and tenor section of the early dance bands was developing into the most effective manifestation of saxophones hunting in a pack; the two altos, two tenors and baritone section which was to become the supremely drilled machine of the great swing bands of the 30's and 40's.

The Saxophone Section of the Ted Heath Band, pictured on board the Queen Mary, prior to a USA tour in March 1956.
L–R: Ken Kiddier (baritone), Ronnie Chamberlain (alto), Les Gilbert (alto), Red Price (tenor) and Henry Mackenzie (tenor)

15

From this environment the saxophone emerged as the great solo jazz instrument we know so well today; inextricably linked with the legendary jazzmen in a symbiotic fusion with their tones, styles and personalities. The most important of these will be discussed in more detail in a later chapter.

Meanwhile, one other definition of terms. Life was simpler in the nineteenth century, but we've now reached the point in time where we have to start discussing the divergence of musical styles: 'jazz' and . . . what? The favourite term is 'classical', but I consider 'classical saxophone' to be a misleading term. After all, 'classical' music finished just about the time the saxophone was being invented, and the 'romantic' era started, consequently no original 'classical' music was ever written for the saxophone.

Some say 'legitimate'. In rejecting this term I can do no better than to quote a remark made by the great jazzman Phil Woods in my presence in Baltimore in 1980. He said, "I don't dig this term 'legit saxophonist' . . . like, what am I . . . chopped liver??"

I prefer the term 'straight'. This is not to imply that jazz is in any way 'bent', but, I think, best defines non-jazz playing as 'straight ahead' reading of the music exactly as written, without jazz inflections or improvisation. So, for the rest of this book I will divide music into three categories; straight, jazz and commercial, the last to include shows, movie scores, light orchestras, dance bands and pop groups.

The turn of the century saw the birth of the Frenchman who was to become the most influential pioneer of the revival of straight saxophone playing in the 20th century. Marcel René Mule was born in Aube, Normandy on June 21st, 1901. Like most saxophonists of his day, his first experience was in a military band, that of the 5th Infantry Regiment. By 1923, he reached the top of this branch of the profession, becoming solo saxophonist of the Garde Républicaine Band, which position he retained for thirteen years. In 1928 he formed the Garde Républicaine Saxophone Quartet, in 1936 the Paris Saxophone Quartet and, finally, in 1951, the Marcel Mule Saxophone Quartet.

The most important date in Mule's career, and in the entire development of saxophone teaching, is 1942, when the Director of the Paris Conservatoire, Claude Delvincourt, decided to

Marcel Mule

reinstate the saxophone class, defunct, we remember, since the end of Adolphe Sax's Professorship in 1870. Marcel Mule was appointed, and taught there for twenty-six years, being succeeded by Daniel Deffayet in 1968.

In the USA it was mainly Cecil Leeson who kept saxophone teaching going between the wars, with the help of Sigurd Rascher and Larry Teal. After the second World War more and more American universities started to appoint Professors of Saxophone, and the numbers of serious players and teachers increased to the extent that in 1968 the World Saxophone Congress was formed, holding its first meeting in Chicago, and continuing to have them every two years ever since.

In 1969 the British saxophone revival started with the formation of the London Saxophone Quartet, which subsequently played at the third World Saxophone Congress in Toronto, Canada in 1972 and at the fourth in Bordeaux, France in 1974. The London Saxophone Quartet was asked to organise the fifth World Saxophone Congress in London, and it duly took place at the Royal College of Music in 1976, being opened by Marcel Mule and featuring saxophonists from seventeen different countries taking part in fifty-six concerts, at which forty-six new works were premiered!

The ten annual British Woodwind Workshops, also organised by the London Saxophone Quartet between 1973 and 1982, were the first events at which leading international saxophonists taught in Britain. These included James Houlik and Robert Black from the USA, Jean-Marie Londeix from France, Elie Apper and Norbert Nozy from Belgium. In 1976 the Clarinet and Saxophone Society of Great Britain was formed, and is still thriving today.

All British Colleges of Music now have Professors of Saxophone, and one of the most important advances in this country has been the inclusion of saxophone Grade Examinations in the syllabus of the Associated Board of the Royal Schools of Music, following many years of lobbying by a small but determined body of saxophone teachers!

This brings us up to the present day, and the contemporary situation will be dealt with in more detail in the subsequent chapters.

An unusual group at one of the Woodwind Workshops
L–R: Christopher Gradwell (ophicleide), the Author (soprano sarrusophone)
Paul Sargent (bass sarrusophone), Edward (Ted) Planas (tenor
sarrusophone) and James Follan (keyed bugle)

Three
The Saxophone Family

A chart of the normal ranges and transpositions of the six members of the saxophone family available today. Comparable clarinet family transpositions are useful to bear in mind for playing band or clarinet choir parts, although the saxophone lacks the lowest fifth of the clarinet's range. The top of all saxophone ranges can be extended upwards in solo music, but it is advisable to keep to the upper limit shown here for normal band, orchestral or quartet writing.

SIZE OF SAXOPHONE	WRITTEN RANGE	SOUNDING (IN CONCERT PITCH)	SAME TRANSPOSITION AS THE:
SOPRANINO IN Eb			Eb CLARINET
SOPRANO IN Bb			Bb CLARINET
ALTO IN Eb			Eb ALTO CLARINET
TENOR IN Bb			Bb BASS CLARINET (FRENCH NOTATION i.e. TREBLE CLEF)
BARITONE IN Eb			Eb CONTRABASS (CONTRA-ALTO) CLARINET
BASS IN Bb			Bb CONTRA BASS CLARINET

Here are some notes for composers/arrangers using the preceding chart for reference: The six saxophones mentioned are those currently being manufactured. However, do not write for the sopranino or the bass unless you have a specific player in mind. The sopranino is extremely difficult to play in tune and the bass is very expensive, heavy and difficult to carry around. Consequently they are not standard items of a saxophonist's equipment; only a handful of professionals make a speciality of either of these extreme sizes.

All professional saxophonists, however, will nowadays possess the standard quartet of soprano, alto, tenor and baritone. The question of the top F sharp key on the first three and the bottom A extension on the baritone would depend for whom you are writing. Professionals would have these notes, but in a school band, for instance, with cheaper instruments, they could not be guaranteed to be available.

Transposition

A transposing instrument is called by the note which it sounds when playing a written C. When a B♭ saxophone plays a written C it sounds B♭; when an E♭ saxophone plays a written C it sounds E♭. The transposition system enables the player to use the same fingerings on all members of the saxophone family. Some theorists have occasionally questioned this, but it is patently obvious to any practical player that this is an immeasurably better system than that of, say, the recorder, where all the sizes play in concert pitch, so you have to use different fingerings on the descant and tenor from those of the treble and bass.

Note the transposition of the baritone saxophone; this makes it very useful for playing bassoon parts. You just read the bass clef concert pitch part as if it were in treble clef, merely changing the key signature by adding three sharps or subtracting three flats.

Playing The Different Members Of The Saxophone Family

The fingering being the same on all saxophones, there are not many points where the playing of the various sizes differs. One obvious difference is that the bigger the mouthpiece, the more you have to put in your mouth, yet it is amazing how many

21

people changing from alto to tenor do not seem to realise this! I have sometimes had good results with alto pupils who do not put enough mouthpiece in by putting them on baritone for a while, so that when they go back to alto, they open their mouths wider. You need a greater volume of air for the bigger saxophones, of course, but if you put more mouthpiece in, it will facilitate that.

There is one much discussed topic which applies only to the soprano; the eternal controversy over straight body versus curved. Personally, I have never been able to see the point of the curved soprano; saxophones are curved so that you can reach the longer tubes, but the soprano being only the length of the clarinet, why add this complication? A straight tube works better, anyway.

Curved sopranos (even curved sopraninos!) were popular with the Vaudeville saxophone groups of the 20's who used to dance around on stage, so I suppose they wanted to look all the same.

Other advantages of the curved soprano are said to be that you can support it by a sling and, for jazz improvising, you can hear yourself better, as the sound comes back up at you.

If you must use a sling for the soprano, I prefer the slightly curved detachable crook which now comes with some of the straight bodied Japanese sopranos, and gives a better blowing angle. The big danger of using a sling at all on the soprano is that it makes you blow it at a downwards angle like the clarinet; the soprano should be held up more horizontally, like the oboe. Of course, you have to develop a strong right thumb, but this is the only way to play if you're leading a saxophone quartet, giving downbeats and cutoffs.

B♭ Soprano and
E♭ Sopranino

The alto controversy is about whether the instrument should be held between the legs or down the right side when playing sitting down. Down the right side is best, as modern instruments are built on the slant, and it gives a better angle for the mouthpiece to go into the mouth. Sometimes, however, you have to play it between your legs for logistic reasons. I remember, for instance, doing a show in a cramped pit, doubling alto and baritone. The baritone stood by my right leg on its stand, so I had to hold the alto between my legs. In this case, the thing to avoid is resting the bell on the seat of the chair, which leads to the even sloppier position of resting the forearms on the thighs. Sit up and keep the weight of the instrument on the sling.

E♭ Alto

The tenor can only be played down the right side, but it is amazing what contorted positions some tenor players manage to twist themselves into! I am often moved to enquire of my tenor pupils, 'And who are we today, then? . . . QUASIMODO or RICHARD THE THIRD?'

Again, sit up straight, with your head vertical. Turn the crook and twist the mouthpiece, so that it comes to your mouth; don't bend yourself to the mouthpiece.

The problem with the baritone is how best to support its weight; the ball and socket type stand is the most practical, especially for doubling. If you prefer a sling, it is well worth experimenting with some of the harness style slings now on the market, as they spread the weight more efficiently than the usual neckstrap.

A word on slings in general; you must choose one which slides up and down easily, but stays put when you've got it to the position you want. Bad playing posture is so often caused by the old leather 'dog-lead' style slings, which are not easily adjustable.

Eb Baritone   Bb Tenor

THE LONDON SAXOPHONE QUARTET (1969–85)
L–R: Hale Hambleton (alto), Paul Harvey (soprano), David Lawrence
(baritone and bass) and Christopher Gradwell (tenor)

SAXPAK is a septet using the whole saxophone family, which was formed
in 1986 by the arranger, Ted White. The personnel is:
back row, l–r: Tim Holmes (alto), John Harle (soprano), Peter Davis
(sopranino), Peter Ripper (alto) and Stan Sulzmann (tenor).
Kneeling in front: David White (bass) and Andrew Findon (baritone)

COMPARISON OF THE F–C FAMILY WITH THE Eb–Bb FAMILY
L–R: F alto (René Guénot: Peter Ripper collection)
Modern Yamaha Eb alto (author's collection)

COMPARISON OF THE F–C FAMILY WITH THE E♭–B♭ FAMILY
L–R: C 'Melody' (Buescher: Peter Ripper collection)
B♭ tenor (Selmer 'cigar cutter': 1933, author's collection)

The Obsolete Members Of The Saxophone Family

Adolphe Sax envisaged the saxophone as two groups; the Eb/Bb family, wide bore, full toned military band instruments, especially suitable for outdoor playing, and a narrower bore F/C family, pitched a tone higher (therefore smaller) more discreet sounding, for orchestral playing.

Probably because the saxophone was immediately successful as a military band instrument, the F/C family never really seemed to get off the ground. The composers who wrote the early orchestral saxophone parts nearly always used the Eb/Bb family, presumably because they were, even then, more readily available, Sax having made a lot more of them for military band use.

This is how the situation stands with the F/C family:

The Sopranino in F: Completely obsolete, if it ever existed at all!

The Soprano in C: Only a few old ones around. It would be a very useful instrument if manufactured with modern techniques. It is the only saxophone which sounds written notes at concert pitch, and can play oboe parts exactly as written.

The Bb soprano is the saxophone which modern manufacturers have improved the most, elongating and narrowing the top of the bore to improve the intonation of the top register, which is dreadfully sharp on older instruments. Unfortunately, all C sopranos have the old, wild intonation.

The Alto in F: Very rare indeed.

The Tenor in C: This is the famous 'C Melody Saxophone' which was an extremely popular solo instrument in the 1920's, being the speciality of Rudy Wiedoeft and several other stars of the day. It is a concert pitch instrument, but sounds an octave lower. Much of its popularity was due to amateurs using it to play straight off song copies, without having to transpose. There are still quite a few around, which are much sought after by enthusiasts.

The big problem is, if you come across one, has it still got its own mouthpiece? If not, it's very difficult to play in tune; alto mouthpieces are too small and tenor mouthpieces are too big.

The Baritone in F: Extremely rare, virtually obsolete.

The Bass in C: This is the one that Sax made first, but nobody's seen one since!

There are a few E♭ Contrabass Saxophones around, sounding an octave below the baritone, but their number is probably in single figures.

Adolphe Sax's 1846 patent mentions some very strange ones, such as an E♭ tenor (but he probably meant what he later called the alto) and a G contrabass, which could also be made in A♭. This one probably only ever existed on Adolphe's drawing board!

E♭ Contrabass Saxophone by the Italian makers Orsi being played by Paul Sargent. Onlookers include the composer, Carey Blyton (left background) Peter Ripper of the LSQ, and Woodwind Workshop participants

Four
The Parts of the Saxophone and its Acoustics

The Mouthpiece

No other wind instrument can be so totally changed by different mouthpieces as the saxophone. One night you might go to a symphony concert and hear the straightest possible saxophonist playing one of the orchestral solos such as *L'Arlésienne* or *Pictures from an Exhibition*. The next night you might go to a pop concert and hear a rock saxophonist playing edgy, screaming solos with an electric band. These two players could not possibly sound more different, yet they could both be playing on exactly the same model of instrument. It is the MOUTHPIECE which produces the contrasting sounds.

There are two main parts of the mouthpiece which affect the tone; the lay (sometimes called the facing) which is the opening between the reed and the tip of the mouthpiece, and the tone chamber inside.

Mouthpieces are nearly always marked with a letter or a number to tell you the width of the lay. Unfortunately there is no standard system for this; all the different manufacturers have their own system. Some use numbers, in which case No. 1 would be the closest (narrowest) going up to perhaps 7 or 8 for the widest (the most open). Others use letters, A being the closest, going up alphabetically to F or G for the widest. Some makers have other systems which are less obvious, so you have to consult their publicity literature to find out what they mean.

If you are just starting on the saxophone it is vital to use a mouthpiece with a medium close lay, about C in letters or 3 in numbers. This will start you blowing the right way; a very close

A STRAIGHT MOUTHPIECE

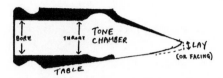

Note the *round* tone chamber
and the close (narrow) lay

A JAZZ MOUTHPIECE

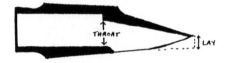

Note the corners
in the throat
and the open (wide) lay

lay will speak too easily, the reed might close up, and you would play very flat in the upper register. Too wide a lay would cause you to grip too hard with your jaw to get a sound, and the bottom notes would not speak at all.

Beginners also make better progress on a mouthpiece with a round chamber inside, as this gives more resistance, or 'back pressure' and develops proper air support. There is no indication about this on the outside of a mouthpiece; you just have to hold it up to the light and look through it.

The 'edge' required for jazz and rock playing is imparted by various corners and projections in the throat of the mouthpiece. There are so many different degrees of these on the market now, that the only way to find which suits you best is to try as many as possible.

31

The material the mouthpiece is made of does not affect the sound as much as the lay and the tone chamber. Metal mouthpieces are very much more expensive than the usual black 'hard rubber' or ebonite ones. Glass mouthpieces are also available, but so far are not as widely used on the saxophone as on the clarinet. I have found metal mouthpieces to be good for playing the altissimo register, but when playing softly, they tend to 'fry' a lot, owing to the breath condensing more on the colder metal, I suppose.

Once you can play the instrument, the kind of mouthpiece you use must be dictated by your musical taste. Most professional players, engaged in a variety of styles of work, will have several different mouthpieces. Bear in mind that it is possible to play jazz on a straight mouthpiece, but it is rather hard work, and will sound a bit 'polite'. On the other hand it is impossible to play straight music properly on a jazz mouthpiece, except perhaps contemporary music of the avant garde school.

Jazz mouthpieces are not necessarily louder; they just have more edge. Round chamber straight mouthpieces can carry just as well in a big hall because the sound has more centre. The only way to get the bottom notes on a wide lay mouthpiece is with a 'huffing' sub-tone (à la Ben Webster). Although this is a most effective sound for jazz ballad playing, it is not suitable for straight music. Therefore a closer lay is necessary to get bottom notes with a full, centred sound.

Most books and articles on mouthpieces feature a chart of lays and other dimensions, but I consider it is more important to have a chart of musical styles and to select your mouthpiece according to the appropriate tone for the music.

The Reed

The saxophone uses a single reed made from the bamboo Arundo Donax, which is mostly grown in the South of France. Moisten the flat side of the reed and place it against the table of the mouthpiece; the thin tip of the reed should come nearly level with the tip of the mouthpiece, with just a thin line of black showing above it. If the reed is very slightly soft it may be pushed

STYLE OF MUSIC:	WIDTH OF LAY:
Rock and Pop styles with electric band.	OPEN
Solo Jazz with rhythm section.	
5 Sax Section in a Big Band.	
Contemporary Straight Music: (avant garde, multiphonics, altissimo etc.) Solo or Quartet.	
Section playing in a Symphonic Wind Band.	
General straight solo playing, with piano or orchestra.	
General Saxophone Quartets.	
LEARNING THE INSTRUMENT.	
Orchestral playing, (with strings).	
Transcriptions of Baroque flute and oboe Sonatas etc.	CLOSE

a little higher, level with the mouthpiece tip; if slightly hard it may be moved lower, showing a little more black. There are no hard and fast rules for what strength of reed to use. As with mouthpieces, the various makers do not have a standard grading system, although they mostly stick to numbers, usually 1 for the softest to about 5 for the hardest, some having half grades in between each number. It is the ratio of the reed strength to the mouthpiece lay which gives different blowing results; generally a close lay will need a harder reed, and a more open lay a softer reed.

To make a reed harder you can clip a thin sliver off the tip with a reed cutter, and to make one softer you scrape a small amount off with a knife, emery paper or 'Dutch rush', a kind of abrasive grass. Only scrape the shaded area, leaving a backbone:

Some people prefer to soften a reed by rubbing the flat side on fine emery paper stuck to a flat glass plate.

To straighten a reed which has gone crinkled at the tip; put it on the mouthpiece, push the other end of the mouthpiece against the palm of your hand and suck the air out of the mouthpiece. The vacuum thus formed pulls the reed against the lay, until the spring in the reed gradually pulls it open again with a popping sound. This operation is good for the reed, and also tests whether the sides of your mouthpiece are even.

Always take the reed off when you finish playing; dry it and wipe out the mouthpiece carefully, but not rubbing the lay, which can be worn down in time. You can either put the reed back on the mouthpiece or keep it flat in a reedguard; if you do the latter, the reed will probably start to work sooner the next time you play it.

The Ligature

There are innumerable different kinds of ligature (which holds the reed on the mouthpiece) on the market today, all claiming to make a wonderful difference to your sound. It doesn't really matter too much which sort you use as long as you observe these two rules: Push the ligature well down onto the mouthpiece, so you can see the guide line (if your mouthpiece has one) above it. The ligature should be halfway down the thick part of the reed. And: Don't do the screws up too tightly; the poor old reed has to be able to vibrate!

I prefer one where the screws are on top of the mouthpiece, because screws underneath tend to come near the chin, and sometimes inhibit beginners from putting enough mouthpiece into their mouths. The 'Rovner' ligature, made of leather type material, only has one screw, and it doesn't matter how tightly you do it up, as the material around the reed is resilient, and does not inhibit the vibration.

The Crook

The cork at the top of the crook, over which the mouthpiece fits, is extremely important, as the tuning of the whole instrument is regulated there. As soon as you get a new saxophone, or have the crook of an old one recorked, find the position of the mouthpiece on the crook where the instrument is in tune (push on to raise the pitch, pull off to lower it) and mark it with a pencil ring around the cork.

I always use a B♭ tuning fork for the alto or baritone; not because the note B♭ has any magical qualities, but for the mundane reason that B♭ concert is G on an E♭ saxophone, and you can play G with just your left hand while pinging the tuning fork with your right. If you tune to an A fork you have to keep putting it down to put your right middle finger on for F sharp. On the soprano or tenor it doesn't matter; you play B with an A fork or C with a B♭ fork, both left hand notes.

If the cork becomes compressed with wear and the mouthpiece feels loose at its in tune position, wind some thread or

35

dental floss around the cork as a temporary measure until you can get it recorked. Always keep the cork well greased, so that you can retune easily.

At the other end of the crook a metal joint fits into the top of the main body of the saxophone. Always make sure the screw at the top of the body is loosened before you put the crook in; if you force it in or pull it out with the screw tight, you could bend the crook. When the crook is in place, tighten the screw. If the crook is still loose when the screw is tight, it needs the attention of a skilled repairman; a temporary measure is to apply a little clear nail varnish to the joint, which keeps it from swivelling round for a while.

Pads And Springs

These two components of the saxophone are not easily visible, but are vital to the efficient functioning of the instrument. Saxophone keys are divided into two categories; closed standing and open standing. Closed standing keys are those which are held closed by a spring when the instrument is at rest; you open the key with your finger pressing against the tension of the spring, and when you release the key, the spring's tension closes it again.

Open standing keys are held away from the hole by spring tension when the instrument is at rest. You close the key with finger pressure and when you release it the spring's tension opens it again.

Getting the bottom notes on the saxophone depends on three factors; not having too wide a lay mouthpiece; all pads making an airtight seal with the rims of the holes; and strong springs on the closed standing keys, holding the pads firmly shut.

The most troublesome spring/pad situation is always G sharp (little finger left hand). All saxophonists are used to the experience of fingering this note, only to hear a G natural! This is because the G sharp pad is opened by spring tension alone, and if the spring is slightly weak, or the pad is at all sticky, it will remain closed.

The temporary cure is either to dust the pad with pad powder, or to clean the pad with lighter fuel or dry cleaning fluid. It is inadvisable to try to alter any spring tensions yourself, as there are many places on the saxophone mechanism where the ratios of spring tensions are very finely balanced, such as the automatic octave mechanism, and altering one can throw out the balance of all the others. A regular check by a skilled repairman to ensure that all your pads are sealing efficiently is the best way to combat bottom note difficulties.

The Acoustics Of The Whole Tube

When all the holes in the saxophone are closed, the tube works just like a big bugle, except that the notes are produced by a reed and mouthpiece instead of a brass cup mouthpiece. The conical bore tube of the saxophone produces all the harmonic series:

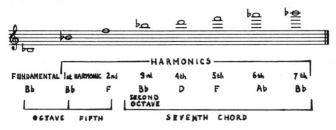

Finger bottom B♭ to close the whole tube, and practise pitching the first three harmonics. The 2nd harmonic (F) will speak more easily than the 1st (B♭). To improve the 1st harmonic, play 'Three Blind Mice' in B♭, all on first harmonics; the 1st harmonic of D is easier to pitch than that of B♭;

You will find that harmonics speak more easily if you don't start the note in the usual way with the tongue on the reed, but with a sort of cough from the throat, backed up by an impulse from the diaphragm. 'HAW' for a lower harmonic, 'HEE' as they get higher. Never use this attack other than for harmonic practice. Practise well known bugle calls, as these are all on the notes of the harmonic series; *The Last Post* is the best one, as it's slow, and gives you time to pitch the harmonics.

Sigurd Rascher had a saxophone without any holes; just the bare tube, especially made to demonstrate the harmonic series. At Summer Music Camps he would go out to the flagpole at dusk and blow *Taps* (the American equivalent of *The Last Post*) on it as the Stars and Stripes was lowered.

THE LAST POST
(Finger bottom B♭ throughout)

You can do these harmonic exercises a semitone higher each time on all the notes up to D^1:

The seventh chord of harmonics 3, 4, 5, 6 and 7 is the basis of the altissimo register. This type of practice is to develop 'tube control', which benefits your sound, intonation, breath control, low notes, high notes, dynamics; in fact everything except tonguing and finger technique.

The middle part of the body, from D^1 to C sharp^2 is where we are most aware of the saxophone overblowing octaves, as these two registers have identical fingering, the lower being fundamentals, the upper first harmonics assisted by opening the octave key:

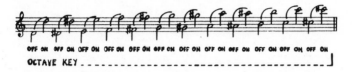

Early saxophones had two separate octave keys, but for many years the automatic octave mechanisms has been standard. To see how this works, finger

  (all left hand plus octave key with left thumb)
Lift and drop third finger, left hand, playing G and A

See how the upper octave hole on the crook opens for A and closes for G. The lower octave hole on the main body of the instrument, level with the top F hole, opens for G and closes for A. This lower octave hole is in a compromise position; it's at a good point for E, F and F sharp, but rather too low for G and too high for D. This is why those are often unstable notes in the 2nd register, especially D, which is prone to fly up to the next harmonic, A. The theoretically perfect saxophone would have at least FOUR octave holes; this has been tried, but, as you can imagine, it proved to be much too mechanically complicated.

Five
Saxophone Fingering

This is a diagram of a saxophone stripped of all mechanism except the keys and 'pearls' which you actually touch with your fingers.

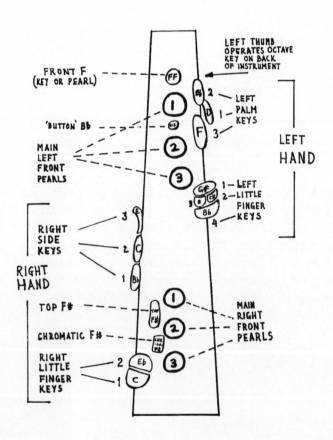

Saxophone Fingerings Divided Into Registers

The fingering of the saxophone can be divided into five very distinct registers; the bottom register; four notes all on little finger keys; the lower register and the upper register, which have exactly the same fingerings except for the addition of the octave key for the upper; the top register, five notes on the palm keys and side keys; and the altissimo register, which is based on harmonics.

THE BOTTOM REGISTER

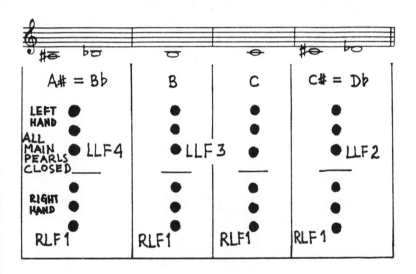

Abbreviations: LLF = left little finger
RLF = right little finger
Enharmonic notes are given for sharps and flats
Note that the C key (RLF 1) stays down for all these notes

The Lower And Upper Registers

Add the octave key with the left thumb for the upper register; otherwise the fingering is exactly the same for both these octaves.

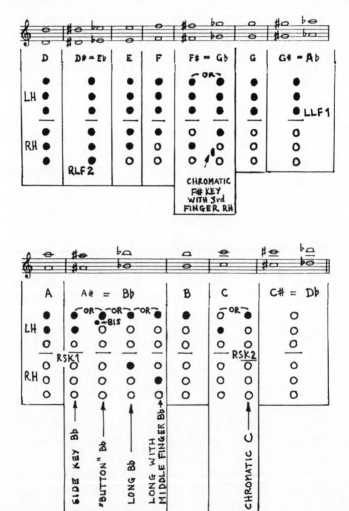

Abbreviation: RSK = right side key

The Top Register

All with left thumb depressing the Octave Key:

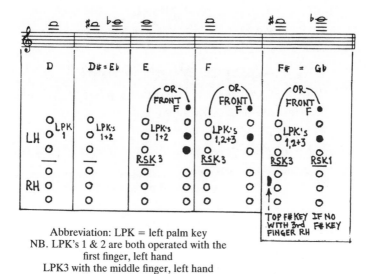

Abbreviation: LPK = left palm key
NB. LPK's 1 & 2 are both operated with the
first finger, left hand
LPK3 with the middle finger, left hand

Before attempting to get the altissimo register it is necessary to have a thorough knowledge of the main part of the instrument. These are some important fingerings which are often incorrectly used:

The Four Fingerings For B♭

On the original saxophone there was only one fingering for B♭ s 2 and 3: left hand 1st and 2nd fingers plus right side key 1. This is the main B♭ fingering and should be used for all scalic passages. The other three B♭ fingerings were added later to facilitate certain arpeggios, so it is important to know what they are for. 'Button' B♭, called 'Bis' B♭ in France, is where the first finger LH depresses both its usual B pearl AND the little pearl below it. This is for arpeggios going from G to B♭, i.e. E♭ major, G minor, B♭ diminished etc.

ALL BUTTON B♭

43

'Long B♭' with first finger is where the B♭ hole is closed by remote control, by the first finger RH. This is for arpeggios of B♭, going from F to B♭:

ALL LONG B♭'s WITH 1st FINGER

Long B♭ with middle finger is the same idea, but with middle finger RH, for arpeggios of E♭ minor, F sharp major etc.

KEEP MIDDLE FINGER RH DOWN
ALL THE TIME

Chromatic Fingerings

It is important to use the chromatic F sharp key and the chromatic C key (RSK 2) for smooth chromatic passages:

K   K   SK   SK

Trills

Do not trill across the registers; use palm keys for these trills:

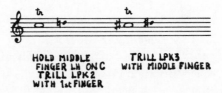

HOLD MIDDLE   TRILL LPK3
FINGER LH ON C   WITH MIDDLE FINGER
TRILL LPK2
WITH 1st FINGER

The saxophone has what is called an 'articulated G sharp' which means you can play this trill holding down the G sharp key (LLF 1) all the time:

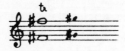

Improving Open C Sharp

C sharp^2 which is the note sounded by the saxophone as it stands, untouched by any fingers on pearls or keys, is a poor quality note. Acceptable in fast passages, something has to be done to improve it and match it better in tone quality to nearby notes in slow passages, especially when coming down from the upper register. In the following five possible fingerings, note that the octave key is open for all of them, but third finger left hand is also on, so it's the LOWER octave hole which is open. So in this case the octave hole is used to raise the pitch slightly, instead of its usual function of overblowing the octave.

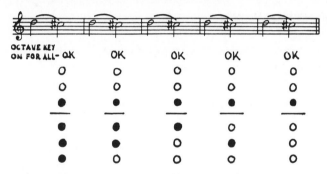

Using Top Register Keys In The Lower Register

These fingerings are sometimes used for very soft passages; these notes, D^2, E♭ (D sharp)^2, and E^2, are very resonant when played with the usual upper register fingerings. These fingerings using palm and side keys have a much more subdued timbre:

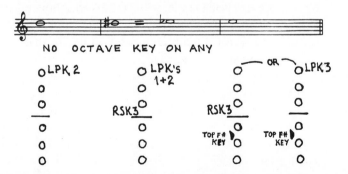

45

All the left little finger keys are coupled together, so any one of them will play G sharp (Ab) if the right hand is off. So you can play all these intervals without moving your left little finger:

LLF 4   LLF 3   LLF 2

The Altissimo Register

These notes are not so much dependent on fingerings as on the ability to pitch harmonics, as described in the previous chapter. The simplest way to approach them at first is by overblowing 6ths, on the normal top register notes:

C# – A#   D – B   Eb – C   E – C#   F – D   F# – D#

These are not very well in tune, so once you can get them, you have to start experimenting with fingerings. The hardest part of the altissimo to control is the bridge notes, G and G sharp. A great variety of fingerings is possible for all altissimo notes, and they differ on the various sizes of saxophones and on different makes. The following chart gives the most used for the first fourth of the altissimo register on Alto. Approach them as written, with a major chord, as this helps you get the pitch in your ear. Always use the front fingerings for E and F when going into the altissimo register.

There is, theoretically, no upward limit to the range of the saxophone; after that it's just a matter of working out controlled squeaks. Don't forget:

A SQUEAK IS JUST A HARMONIC IN THE WRONG PLACE!

SOME ALTISSIMO FINGERINGS

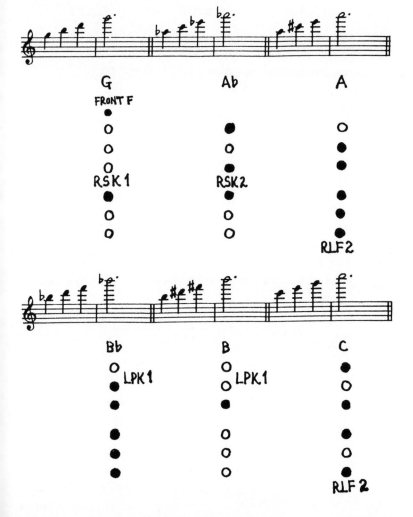

Six
Tone Production

Many books on wind instruments show physiologically accurate diagrams of the human respiratory system in one section of the book, and, separately, in a different section, as if there were no connection between the two, they show a scientifically accurate diagram of the bore of the instrument.

Knowing the exact dimensions of your respiratory system and the bore of your instrument is very interesting, but it does not make you play any better. I present, therefore, my 'primitive art' representation of the symbiotic relationship between body and instrument which is what tone production is all about.

Tone comes from the lower part of your trunk, which should feel onion-shaped when playing, even if it's not! Forget your lungs; everything worthwhile happens lower than that. Pitch is controlled by the throat and oral cavity. The lips are merely an airtight seal between the tube inside you and the saxophone tube.

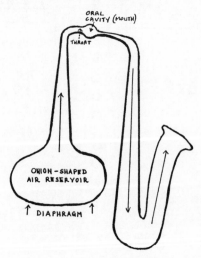

Breathing

Before starting a note it's first necessary to fill yourself up with air. When playing any wind instrument a sufficient quantity of air can be taken in quickly enough only through the MOUTH. Breathing in through the nose is the worst possible habit on any wind instrument. Excess air can be expelled through the nose before taking another breath, but all breathing IN must be through the MOUTH.

The author and a pupil demonstrating a remedial technique to cure breathing in through the nose; wearing a swimmer's nose clip, with the spring tension reduced, so that you can still breathe OUT through the nose, but not IN

Before taking the first breath, put the mouthpiece in your mouth. There is much talk of 'forming an embouchure', which in some people's minds seems to mean pulling their bottom lip over their bottom teeth as far in as it will go and gripping the mouthpiece and reed like a rabid bulldog! If you 'form an embouchure' like this on the saxophone it will inhibit the flow of air from your body into the instrument.

Merely open your mouth as if MILDLY SURPRISED. Put the mouthpiece in and rest your top teeth on top of it. Let your top lip touch the top of the mouthpiece in front of your teeth. Your top lip must stay there as if stuck with glue; never lift your top lip to breathe; it's a waste of time, as your top teeth are in the way. I never, ever, want to see your top teeth when you're playing! Breathe like this: drop your bottom jaw, as if DEEPLY SHOCKED, and breathe in as if ABSOLUTELY HORRIFIED.

49

When your lower trunk feels as if it has reached its maximum onion shape, relax your bottom jaw and allow your bottom lip to

The author pictured PRACTISING WHAT HE PREACHES; dropping the bottom jaw for quick breath, which is the only way to get enough air in quickly

touch the reed, just enough lip covering the bottom teeth so that they don't touch the reed.

Push the reed against the mouthpiece with your tongue, so that it's closed up, and all that air in your onion has nowhere to go. Imagine that your belt has broken, and you have to keep your trousers up by tensing the muscles that control the shape of your onion, so that the air is under maximum blowing pressure, and then take your tongue away from the reed. This is how to start a note without any particular accent; don't strike the reed with the tongue; just remove it and allow the air to flow into the instrument.

It should be warm air; blow onto your hand as if steaming up a mirror before polishing it . . . HUHH . . . not cold air, like blowing a feather off your hand . . . PHEW.

Although this will be mentioned again and in a later chapter on doubling, a comparison here to tone production on the clarinet is the best way to illustrate throat and oral cavity shape. At this point you get a good clarinet sound by blowing UP to the pitch, thinking 'EEEEE'. On the saxophone you get the right sound by blowing DOWN to the pitch, thinking 'AWWWW' (as in AWful, N.B. English pronunciation).

If your throat and oral cavity are the right shape, you should get the following concert pitch notes by blowing just the *mouthpiece and reed alone* of the four main sizes of saxophone:

| SOPRANO | ALTO | TENOR | BARITONE |

Vibrato

When a good centred sound is established over the whole range, it's time to start developing vibrato. Your job as a saxophone player is to be able to produce even vibrato of any required width and any required speed, or to stop the vibrato altogether and produce a perfectly straight note, with a full, centred sound. Anyone who can only play vibrato at one speed or can only play a straight note is not a fully equipped saxophonist. Musical taste eventually dictates where to use vibrato, and at what width and speed.

To gain this control takes the following type of practice: Saxophone vibrato is best done with the lower jaw. I sometimes teach the saxophone to flautists and oboists who already have a well established diaphragm vibrato, and we usually find that this works fairly well on the saxophone, yet I never feel that it is quite as well controlled as jaw vibrato on a single reed instrument.

The jaw, not just the chin but the whole jawbone, right back to the 'hinges' near the ears, must move UP and DOWN, not backwards and forwards. In fact the movement is exactly like eating. Try to make the change of pitch sound like a smooth undulation: ⌒⌒⌒⌒ not jagged: ∧∧∧∧∧∧∧ .

Practise with a regular beat and vibrato in minims, then crotchets, crotchet triplets, quavers, triplets, semiquavers, then a long straight note, then do it all again, at different dynamic levels and in different registers of the instrument.

When you have acquired this physical control, then listen to some great singers, violinists and cellists to get some ideas about how to use vibrato.

Tonguing

I include tonguing under 'Tone Production' because air support is the most important factor. Follow the earlier instructions for starting a note, then, when the note has sounded for a couple of seconds, put your tongue back on the reed, closing it, but keep blowing. Feel the air inside you pressing to get out. Release your tongue again, and let the note speak. Stop it again with the tongue on the reed. It is this silence between the notes when you are maintaining full blowing power, but stopping the reed with your tongue, that is the key to all articulation.

Staccato is when you stop the reed with your tongue immediately the note has spoken, maintaining even air support. The quicker your tongue stops the reed, the quicker you can release the next note, so shortness is the secret of fast staccato.

Double And Triple Tonguing

Double and triple tonguing works very well on the trumpet and the flute; it doesn't work quite so well on single reed instruments, but it's certainly more successful on the saxophone than on the clarinet. The problem is that you are alternating the consonants T and K, (or saying Tuh-Kuh) and the K articulation is not as clear as the T on a single reed. Don't attempt double tonguing until you have mastered single tonguing, so that your T produces a clear note. Then you have to practise the K articulation, or back stroke, where the tongue rebounds from the T, until the K produces the clearest note possible.

Once you can do a good K articulation, there isn't really anything new to learn for triple tonguing, just sorting out your consonants: TKT-TKT-TKT etc. The greatest double and triple tonguer of all time was Rudy Wiedoeft, so if you want to become the Rudy Wiedoeft of the 21st century, I recommend Trevor Wye's 'Practice Book for the Flute', Volume 3, Articulation (Novello). Everything in there, and the exercises for double and triple tonguing, are equally applicable to the saxophone.

Seven
Special Effects

This is a sensitive area, as the saxophone is still trying to live down the awful reputation it acquired in the 1920's, when its incredible flexibility was excessively exploited by many players who put showmanship before musicianship. However, the complete player should know how these effects are obtained, and experimenting with them improves your control. Whether or not you care to display them in public is purely a matter between you and your musical conscience!

The Glissando

Saxophone sound is so 'bendable' that the problem is usually to prevent it doing a glissando where it would be musically inappropriate. All the pitch variation comes from the oral cavity and throat (nothing to do with the lip); basically, think 'AWW' to go down and 'EEE' to come up again. It's much easier to do on first harmonics (upper register) than on fundamentals (lower register).

The glissando can be a useful remedial exercise for somebody who plays flat in the upper register. If you get them to drop the pitch even more, and then slide up again, they eventually slide up further than the pitch where they started, so attaining the right pitch.

The Growl

This is very effective in jazz-rock styles, and is best achieved by singing with your own playing. You don't have to sing the same actual notes you're playing, just follow the shape of the phrase with your voice. The vibration of your vocal chords splits the vibration of the air column in the instrument, providing the growling effect.

Flutter Tonguing

For this effect the tongue is allowed to roll freely in the oral cavity, as in pronouncing the Spanish 'RRRR'. It is the opposite of the glissando, in that it works better in the lower register than in the upper.

Slap Tonguing

Probably the most undesirable of the 1920's effects, but this is the traditional description of how it's done: Place the tongue flat against the reed, and form a cup in the centre of the tongue by muscular contraction.

The cup forms a vacuum with the surface of the reed. Lower the tongue, and the force of the vacuum draws the reed with it. After a moment the natural springiness of the reed reasserts itself, and it springs back into position, striking the lay of the mouthpiece with a slapping sound. If you blow at the same time as the reed hits the lay, the slap and the note amplify one another. It is only really effective on low notes.

Multiphonics

Used quite a lot nowadays as an avant garde effect. The first step in experiments with multiphonics would be trying to make the fundamental and the first harmonic sound simultaneously. Finger a lower register note; make it overblow the octave without using the octave key, by adjusting your oral cavity and throat, then relax just enough so that the fundamental begins to sound again. This is actually very good tube control practice. After that consult some of the innumerable 'Contemporary Techniques for Saxophone' publications which have been produced in the USA, for some fingering suggestions, which are infinitely variable.

The Saxophone Mute

A mute is really only effective on a brass instrument, where all the notes come out through the bell. However, for orchestral playing, one sometimes uses a 'doughnut', a piece of cloth rolled into a circle with a hole in the middle, inserted into the bell. This softens the bottom notes, but you lose the B♭ altogether, of course. For bottom B natural, turn the doughnut sideways.

There is an old trick of dropping a cork (wine bottle size) down the bell. This lodges in the bow of the body, and takes some edge off the bottom notes, but the effect is fairly minimal.

The only saxophone mute I ever saw which affected the whole instrument was at a World Saxophone Congress once. A chap played a piece of his own composition with the saxophone inside a goatskin bag with three holes in it; one at the top, where the mouthpiece poked out, and one either side through which he put his hands to finger the instrument. What did it sound like? As far as I can remember, it sounded like a saxophone being played inside a goatskin bag!

Circular Breathing

This is a technique for taking in air through the nose while still maintaining a playing airflow through the mouth. It is best practised away from the instrument, using a glass of water and a straw. Blow normally through the straw into the water, producing an even bubbling effect. Fill your cheeks with air and keep the bubbles going by pushing the air out of your mouth with cheek pressure. At the same time inhale air through your nostrils. This is easy enough to do in itself, but the difficulty is to achieve the change from normal blowing to cheek blowing and back to normal without interrupting the air flow.

Like any special technique, it is good for you to acquire it, but, personally, I am very doubtful as to its musical desirability. Playing a wind instrument, especially the saxophone, is exactly like singing; the musical shape and intelligibility depend so much on the natural punctuation of the human necessity to take breaths. One hears jazz players who have mastered circular

breathing, showing off their ability continuously, while improvising an unrelenting stream of notes. Jazz, more than any other
style of music, depends for its form on the 'question and answer'
of juxtaposed phrases. If there are no breathing spaces in an
improvisation, it might just as well be played on a synthesiser as
on a human, vocal instrument like the saxophone.

Subtone

A kind of muting effect for the bottom register achieved by
constricting the vibration of the reed with the lip. The bottom lip
is pushed out more than usual so as to cover a larger area of the
reed. The top teeth are brought a little nearer to the tip of the
mouthpiece, so that the gap between reed and lay is reduced.
You then have to blow slightly harder to force the airstream
through this narrower opening.

The technique works best with a wide lay mouthpiece, and is
most effective in producing a breathy tone for use in jazz ballad
playing.

It is not recommended for straight playing, where low notes
should be played with the natural, centred sound. Use of sub-
tone as an easy way to produce bottom notes can become a
habit, giving an inappropriate style to much of one's playing.

As with all these special effects, it is good to know HOW to do
it, but you must also know when NOT to do it!

Eight
Doubling

It goes without saying that the modern saxophonist should be prepared to play any of the saxophone family. An expensive undertaking to equip oneself for, but it can be done gradually, on hire purchase. It's usually best to start with an alto, then a tenor, then either baritone or soprano, depending on what is needed in whatever groups you may be playing with.

But however many saxophones you may possess, your musical activities will always be limited unless you double other members of the woodwind family; clarinet, certainly, and, nowadays, flute as well.

Beginners often ask me which instrument it's best to start on, and I have no hesitation in advising them to start on clarinet. I have taught many saxophonists the clarinet, and many clarinettists the saxophone, and have no doubt that it's better to start on the tighter embouchure, open holed, twelfth overblowing clarinet, and then relax your embouchure and use the upper register fingerings in both octaves with covered holes, on the saxophone.

This is not to say that the saxophone is any easier to play; in fact, in my opinion, it's more difficult than the clarinet to play WELL. Don't forget the main difference between blowing the clarinet and saxophone: on clarinet blow UP to the pitch, 'EEEE', and on saxophone blow DOWN to the pitch, 'AWWW'.

The flute could be added gradually; that's mainly a matter of getting the embouchure and tone production right. It's particularly vital in the case of the flute to start learning it under the guidance of a good teacher. Don't be put off by any of the old wives tales about doubling, like playing the saxophone not being good for your clarinet sound, etc. All doubling is good for you; playing the saxophone does wonders for your diaphragm support on clarinet, and the flute is very compatible with the saxophone.

Then there is the musical consideration; how can you get any early orchestral experience unless you play clarinet or flute? You don't want the first thing you ever play in an orchestra to be one of the big saxophone solos like 'L'Arlésienne' or 'Pictures'. Nowadays all saxophonists have to play transcriptions of Baroque flute sonatas for exams. What an advantage if you've also played the originals on flute!

How else can you obtain first hand experience of the sublime wind music of Mozart except by playing it on the clarinet? Bear in mind that he doesn't even use flutes in most of the Wind Serenades.

The clincher, of course, is if you aspire to be a professional musician; there is no way you can make a living unless you double. Consider all the players who regularly do the saxophone work in the professional orchestras in this country; I can't think of one who doesn't make most of his living on the clarinet.

Consider musical shows; this is where the most doubling of all takes place, especially flute nowadays. Consider teaching; there are not many places where you could just teach saxophone; all schools would require you to teach clarinet and flute, perhaps even oboe and bassoon as well.

Here is a little anecdote to illustrate doubling in the commercial session business. For many years I managed to survive as a single reed 'specialist', which is to say that I only played five different size saxophones and nine different members of the clarinet family. One day a fixer rang and booked me for some recording sessions; giving me the phone number of a well known arranger, he said, 'Ring the arranger nearer the time to find out what instruments he wants you on.'

In due course I did so, and the arranger said, consulting his score, 'Hi, Paul . . . yes, let me see . . . I've got you on . . . er . . . tenor sax . . . er . . . Eb contrabass clarinet . . . and . . . er . . . alto flute, O.K.?'

'I'm terribly sorry', I said, 'but I'm afraid I don't play alto flute.' 'WHAT??' he replied incredulously, 'but EVERYBODY plays alto flute!'

Fortunately, he had time to re-allocate the doublings, but that was when I started practising the flute!

The author with some of his equipment as a single reed 'specialist'!

Nine
The Orchestral Saxophone Repertoire

Many of the earlier orchestral saxophone parts tend to be set piece solos, with very little or no tutti playing to get warmed up on. Therefore it is essential to have prior knowledge of these before arriving at an orchestral rehearsal. Many other orchestral saxophone parts are being written all the time, of course, and you have to rely on your sight reading ability for the new ones. This list is intended to give you some indication of the parts which you would be expected to know in advance.

ALBENIZ: *El Albaicin*, from the suite *Iberia*
Several tenor solos in Spanish style.

BERG, Alban: Violin Concerto
A very important alto part, with plenty to play. At one point you have to double third clarinet for a few bars.
Lulu; an opera and a symphonic suite from the opera.
This is one of the most technically demanding of all orchestral alto parts. It is not sight readable, and needs a lot of practice.

BIZET: *L'Arlésienne*, Suites 1 and 2
This is the best known alto saxophone part of all time. The first big solo in Suite 1 is the most quoted in books on orchestration. The suites are taken from incidental music which Bizet wrote for a play by Alphonse Daudet in 1872. The saxophone represents one of the characters, 'L'Innocent', a rather simple youth with romantic inclinations. The second suite was arranged by Guiraud after Bizet's death, and contains a long saxophone tune, in octaves with the horn.

61

L'ARLÉSIENNE

Eb Alto Saxophone

BRITTEN, Benjamin: *Sinfonia Da Requiem, Our Hunting Fathers, Prince of the Pagodas* and *Billy Budd*.
All of these works by Britten have very important alto parts.

DELIBES: *Sylvia*, ballet.
One number in Act 3 is an alto solo, with lots of soft bottom C's, for which a doughnut is a great help.

KHACHATURIAN: *Sabre Dance* from ballet *Gayaneh*.
Alto plays the slower middle tune in this popular number.

KODALY: *Harry Janos Suite*.
The fourth movement, The Battle and Defeat of Napoleon, has some effective alto solos, especially the Funeral March. Some low B's in the battle section.

MASSENET: *Werther*.
An opera written in 1892, with a very low solo (bottom B's) in Act 3.

BARCAROLLE
from the Ballet "Sylvia"(Act III)

The Saxophone

MILHAUD: *La Création du Monde.*

The alto is used instead of a viola, and it is usual for the saxophone to sit in the string section, where the viola would be.

MOUSSORGSKY/RAVEL: *Pictures From An Exhibition*

In Ravel's orchestration of Moussorgsky's piano suite, the second movement, The Old Castle, is a beautiful alto solo, the best known orchestral saxophone part after *L'Arlésienne*.

THE OLD CASTLE

PROKOFIEV: *Romeo and Juliet*, ballet and two suites from the ballet. *Lieutenant Kije* and *Alexander Nevsky*.

All these works have extremely important tenor saxophone parts. The fourth movement of Lieutenant Kije, Troika (Sleighride) is often played as a separate item, and the tenor is heard playing both well known tunes in it.

Romeo and Juliet

Suite No.2

B♭ Tenor Saxophone

Sergei Prokofiev (1891-1953)

I. The Montagues and the Capulets

II. Juliet, the Little Girl

V. Romeo and Juliet Before Parting

VI. Dance of the Maids from the Antilles

IV. Troika (Lieutenant Kije)

RACHMANINOFF: *Symphonic Dances*
An alto solo in the key of C sharp major.

RAVEL: *Bolero*
Two players are required for this piece; one on soprano and one on tenor. Both play the second of the two Bolero tunes, the tenor first, followed by the soprano playing exactly the same fingerings, but sounding an octave higher, of course. Ravel must have been given some really inaccurate information about the soprano saxophone, because he seemed to think it wouldn't go up to top Eb, and started the second solo on sopranino (in F too; very strange for a master of orchestration like Ravel) but where the sopranino runs out of range as the solo descends he writes for a soprano taking over just for the bottom notes. All totally impractical, of course, so the soprano player just ignores the printed part and looks back to the tenor solo; it's written on a double part, so there's no problem.

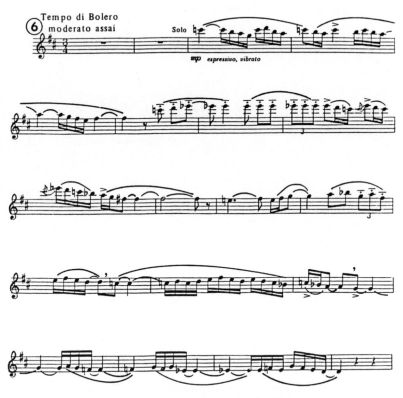

This is what is always actually played, all on the B♭ soprano. It is the written tenor solo; on the tenor it sounds a ninth lower, and on the soprano it sounds a tone lower; exactly the notes which Ravel wanted

SCHOENBERG: *Von Heute Auf Morgen*
An opera with two saxophone parts; one for soprano doubling alto and another for tenor doubling BASS SAXOPHONE IN C! Yes, Adolphe's original! This part is usually transposed onto baritone, as it goes way above the range of the bass anyway.

SHOSTAKOVICH: *The Age of Gold.* Ballet Suite.
A very high soprano solo, going up to top F. The original ballet also has a part for tenor.

The Saxophone

VAUGHAN WILLIAMS: *Job*, A Masque for Dancing
The sixth movement is the famous Dance of Job's Comforters, in
which the alto represents the hypocrites.

Eb Alto Saxophone

DANCE OF JOB'S COMFORTERS

68

Symphony No. 6 in E minor.

A really good tenor part, with plenty of tutti playing to warm up for the exciting solos. The only drawback to this part is that it changes to bass clarinet right at the end of the Symphony for an extremely difficult, high solo. It's usually played by the orchestra's resident bass clarinettist, but if any orchestra ever tries to make you play both parts, ask for a great deal of extra money!

The two main tenor solos from the 3rd Movement

© 1958 Oxford University Press. Reproduced by permission.

Symphony No. 9

Three saxophone parts; two altos and a tenor.

WALTON, William: *Belshazzar's Feast*

This oratorio has an excellent alto part, which, unfortunately, is sometimes played on the cor anglais. I have heard from the lips of Sir William himself that he really wanted the saxophone, but put in the alternative for amateur orchestras who couldn't afford to engage a competent saxophonist.

Facade

Some effective little alto solos in the famous Popular Song and some of the other movements.

Ten
The Saxophone Quartet and its Repertoire

The standard saxophone quartet of soprano, alto, tenor and baritone is undoubtedly the most satisfying medium in which the saxophonist can perform. All the original and important quartets are written for this combination; the two alto, tenor and baritone quartet is mainly a teaching medium; there is a certain amount of material for it, but mostly easy arrangements. So, when we speak of a saxophone quartet, we always mean soprano, alto, tenor and baritone, unless otherwise indicated.

It is sometimes said that the String Quartet is the perfect chamber music medium, and the Saxophone Quartet is the nearest wind equivalent to the string quartet. The standard Wind Quintet of flute, oboe, clarinet, horn and bassoon is a collection of five individuals, while the Clarinet Quartet has never really settled into a standard combination. The Saxophone Quartet offers a true consort of four members of the same family, capable of a homogeneous blend or of displaying their own individual characteristics.

There is a very large repertoire of original works, which, I venture to suggest, contains a larger percentage of attractive material than the saxophone's solo repertoire.

There is also a wealth of arrangements, some more successful than others, of course, but an essential ingredient to the planning of well balanced programmes.

Writing For Saxophone Quartet

My previous comparison with the string quartet is a little dangerous for the composer/arranger. You must bear in mind that the

70

saxophone quartet has a thicker sound than strings, and the full texture of the entire quartet playing simultaneously can become more cloying to the ear than would a string quartet if sustained for too long.

Approach the saxophone quartet, at first, as a quartet of human voices, whose comparative ranges they very closely approximate. Write out parts for a hymn; soprano up a tone, alto up a major sixth, tenor up a ninth into treble clef, and for baritone, just change the bass clef to treble and add three sharps or subtract three flats. This will get you used to the transpositions, and if you've got a quartet available to play it, you can hear the effect when playing in harmony.

Next, write out a four-part Elizabethan Madrigral. Again, the voice parts will fit the saxophone quartet like a glove, and you will hear a more contrapuntal effect.

I suggest that you go no further with four part material as an arranging exercise at this point. If you were now to transpose a string quartet note for note, it would be overwritten for saxophone quartet. The best next step would be to arrange a Baroque keyboard piece (Scarlatti or Couperin, for example) which is mainly in two parts, with occasional chords. Try to divide the florid two part counterpoint between the four saxophones so that each has an interesting part.

Then try some piano music with very thick chords; Ravel, Debussy or jazz, and practise deciding which notes you can leave out of each chord while still preserving the character of the harmony. After all this you should be ready to try your own saxophone quartet compositions.

Playing In A Saxophone Quartet

When you start a quartet, the first step is to get used to listening to one another, playing chords and adjusting your intonation. As I suggested for arrangers and composers, your best starting material is hymns. Why have so many good brass players started in Salvation Army Bands? All that hymn playing, of course; the very best tone practice you can have.

QUATUOR

I Partie

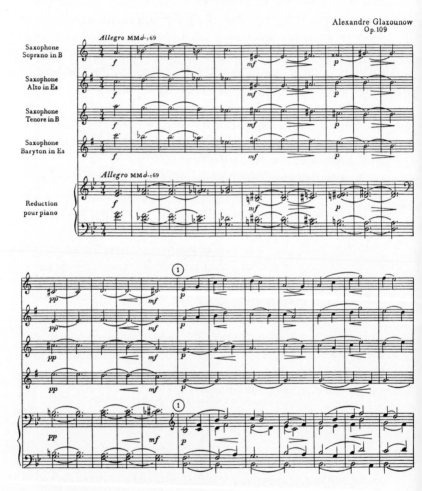

The opening of the Glazounov Quartet, the piano reduction under the score illustrating the transpositions of a soprano, alto, tenor and baritone quartet.

SWING 5

for Five Saxophones (AATTB)

COLIN COWLES

An example of Big Band Sax Section writing, for two altos, two tenors and baritone. The parallel voicings are typical of the style, which is less contrapuntal than SATB quartet writing

73

With four copies of Hymns Ancient and Modern and a little mental effort you can save yourself a lot of writer's cramp. Why not train your quartet to play straight from the hymnbooks? Quite easy for soprano and baritone; soprano adds two sharps, subtracts two flats and plays up a tone. Baritone, as I said before, just reads in treble clef, adding three sharps or subtracting three flats. Harder for alto and tenor, admittedly. Alto up a sixth, add three sharps or subtract three flats. Although tenor is really up a ninth, I actually think of it as up a tone in bass clef, add two sharps, subtract two flats. Maybe this all sounds rather complicated, but you can soon get used to it. The main thing with transposition is to get yourself firmly established in the new key, and hymns are very tonal, with very few accidentals. The slower you play them, the more good they will do your balance and intonation. Start every rehearsal with a hymn; play several verses, at contrasting dynamic levels, one verse completely straight, others with varying speeds of vibrato.

Play plenty of transcriptions of early music; madrigals for part playing, but also even earlier instrumental consort music. This was all written for any available consort; recorders, shawms, crumhorns, viols etc. Had saxophones existed in medieval times they would have been a favourite consort, and, in my opinion, this period of music is the most effective of all to transcribe for saxophone quartet.

The following list of music for saxophone quartet is by no means everything ever written for the medium; that would take up a whole book in itself. It is a selection of publications which I know to be effective from personal use, and which are, at the time of writing, readily available. It would, hopefully, form the basis of a good library from which an active saxophone quartet could devise quite a lot of varied, balanced programmes.

A Selection Of Saxophone Quartet Repertoire

Technically easy pieces suitable for a starting quartet:

Original Works

BLYTON, Carey: *Dance Variations* (Maurer), *In Memoriam Scott Fitzgerald* (Berben), *Pantomime* (Roberton), *In Memoriam*

74

Django Reinhardt (Berben), *Saxe Blue* (Berben), *What Then Is Love?* (Roberton), *Patterns* (composer), *Flying Birds* (composer).

All these works have recently been recorded by the Phoenix Saxophone Quartet on Upbeat URCD 106. These and many other MS works can be obtained from the composer: Carey Blyton, 55 Goldsel Road, Swanley, Kent BR8 8HA.

COWLES, Colin: *A Very First Saxophone Quartet Book* (Studio Music). The best book available for a beginning quartet. It includes a tuning test and six very easy but attractive pieces. The score has a piano reduction under the parts, which is extremely useful for teachers.

HARVEY, Paul: *The Harfleur Song* (Novello).

An original piece in medieval style, written as a sequel to The Agincourt Song.

NESTICO, Sammy: *A Study in Contrasts*.

Easy Arrangements:

COHEN, Paul: *The Renaissance Book* (Galaxy). *Songs and dances from the Court of Henry VIII*. This album is particularly useful because it includes four trios, one minus soprano, one minus alto, one minus tenor and one minus baritone.

HARVEY, Paul: *The Agincourt Song* (Novello) Two Albums of Quartets in the Chester Saxophone Series (Chester/Music Sales).

JOPLIN, Scott: A large number of Rags published by Studio Music.

PIERNÉ, Gabriel: *Chanson D'Autrefois, Chanson De Gran'Maman*, La Veille de L'Ange Gardien and *Marche Des Petits Soldats De Plomb* (Leduc).

Original Works of Medium Difficulty:

AMOS, Keith: Four Society Dances, *Saxifrage* (CMA).

CLÉRISSE, Robert: *Cache-Cache, Caravan, Chanson du Rouet*, Introduction et Scherzo, *Sérénade Melancholique* (Leduc).

COWLES, Colin: Five Short Saxophone Quartets, Set Of Four in Popular Style, (Studio Music).

HARVEY, Paul: Seven Saxophonian Folk Dances (Kjos).

JACOB, Gordon: Quartets nos. 1 and 2. (Emerson).

75

SHORT, Michael: Four Fantasies (Studio Music).

SINGELÉE Jean-Baptiste: Premier Quatuor Op. 53 (1857) (Molenaar). This is one of the earliest quartets, and one of the few original quartets in late classical style.

Arrangements Of Medium Difficulty:

ALBENIZ: *Trois Pièces* (Leduc).

GERSHWIN, arr. Wood: *American in Paris* (Saxtet).

HARVEY, Paul: Suite from *Acis and Galatea* by Handel (Studio). *Celtic Collage* and *Robert Burns Suite* (Novello).

IBERT, Jacques: *Histoires* (Leduc).

RAVEL, arr. Wood: *Bolero* (Saxtet).

ROSSINI, arr. Wood: *Largo Al Factotum* (Saxtet).

WEILL, Kurt: Music from the *Threepenny Opera*, arr. John Harle (Universal).

Difficult Original Works:

ABSIL, Jean: Suite on Roumanian Themes, Pièces en Quatuor, Quatuor, Op. 31 (Leduc).

BOZZA, Eugène: Andante and Scherzo, Nuages (Leduc).

CORDELL, Frank: *Gestures* (Emerson), *Patterns* (Novello).

DAMASE, Jean-Michel: Quatuor (Lemoine).

DEDRICK, Chris: *Sensitivity* (Kendor).

DESENCLOS, Alfred: Quatuor (Leduc).

DUBOIS, Pierre-Max: Quatuor, Variations (Leduc).

FRANÇAIX, JEAN: PETITE QUATUOR (SCHOTT).

GLAZOUNOV, Alexander: Quartet Op. 109 (Belaieff)

KARLINS, M. William: Quartets Nos. 1 & 2. (Seesaw).

PATTERSON, Paul: Diversions (Weinberger).

PIERNÉ, Gabriel: Introduction et Variations sur une Ronde Populaire.

PIERNÉ, Paul: *Trois Conversations* (GB).

READE, Paul:Quartet (Simrock).

RUSHBY-SMITH, John: Quartet (Simrock).

RIVIER, Jean: Grave et Presto (GB).

SCHMITT, Florent: Quatuor Op. 102 (Durand).

WOOD, Nigel: *Rotunda* (Saxtet).

WOODS, Phil: Three Improvisations (Kendor).

The most important 'classics' of the saxophone quartet repertoire, which all quartets should have in their library, and work on regularly, even if they are a long way from performance standard are:

The GLAZOUNOV: the Canzona and Variations is often played as a separate item, and is more approachable than the rest of the work.

The FRANÇAIX: the second movement is an alto solo with tenor and baritone accompaniment, while the soprano is tacet.

The SCHMITT: an extremely difficult work, very overwritten.

All English Saxophone Quartets should play the two Gordon Jacob quartets as much as possible, because they are the most important English contribution to the medium, apart from being delightful and approachable works, which are always a great success with audiences.

All these quartets can be obtained from:
June Emerson Wind Music, Ampleforth, Yorks, YO6 4HF.

THE LONDON SAXOPHONE QUARTET (1969–85)
L–R: Christopher Gradwell (tenor), David Lawrence (baritone),
Paul Harvey (soprano) and Hale Hambleton (alto)

Eleven
The Saxophone's Solo Repertoire

There are three works for alto saxophone and orchestra which are heard in concert halls enough to be called the 'classics' of the instrument; the Ibert Concertino Da Camera, the Glazounov Concerto and the Debussy Rhapsody. The first two were both written for Sigurd Rascher. Jacques Ibert's Concertino Da Camera of 1935 is so called because it is scored for a chamber orchestra of eleven instruments; wind quintet, string quartet, double bass and trumpet. Alexander Glazounov's Concerto in E♭ Op. 109 was written in 1934 and is scored for strings.

A wealthy American amateur saxophonist, Mrs Elise Hall, commissioned Claude Debussy to write a work for her in 1901. Debussy's heart doesn't seem to have been in the project, because he produced nothing until 1911, when Mrs Hall received a short score. Debussy died in 1918, and his student, Roger Ducasse, orchestrated the work, which was finally premiered in 1919.

There are many other works for solo saxophone and orchestra, of course; here is a selection of them.

Soprano And Orchestra

VILLA LOBOS, Heitor: Fantasia (Sony). This is a wonderful work, scored for Strings and Horns. If it were for alto instead of soprano, it would be one of the 'classics'. Personally, I like it better than any of the 'big three' alto works.

HARVEY, Paul: Concertino (Maurer). Scored for the same accompaniment (eleven instruments) as the Ibert. Dedicated to Paul Brodie.

COWLES, Colin: Elegy. A one movement work scored for string orchestra.

Christopher Gradwell conducting a rehearsal for the first performance of
Paul Harvey's Soprano Concertino, with the composer as soloist.

Alto And Orchestra Or Wind Band

BINGE, Ronald: Concerto (Weinberger)

BENNETT, Richard Rodney: Concerto (Novello)

COATES, Eric: Saxo-Rhapsody (Studio Music) Written for Sigurd
Rascher in 1936.

CRESTON, Paul: Concerto Op. 26 (Schirmer).

DAHL, Ingolf: Concerto (Wind Band).

DAMASE, Jean-Michel: Concertstück (Leduc).

DUBOIS, Pierre-Max: Concertstück, Divertissement (Leduc).

GRUNDMAN, Clare: Concertante (Wind Band) (B & H).

HARVEY, Paul: Concertino (Maurer).

JACOB, Gordon: Miscellanies (Emerson) Original with Wind
Band, composer's own orchestration with strings. Written in
1976 for Paul Harvey.

LEESON, Cecil: Concertino (Southern).

MARTIN, Frank: Ballade (Universal).

MILHAUD, Darius: Scaramouche (Salabert).

TATE, Phyllis: Concerto (OUP).

VELLONES, Pierre: Concerto (Lemoine).

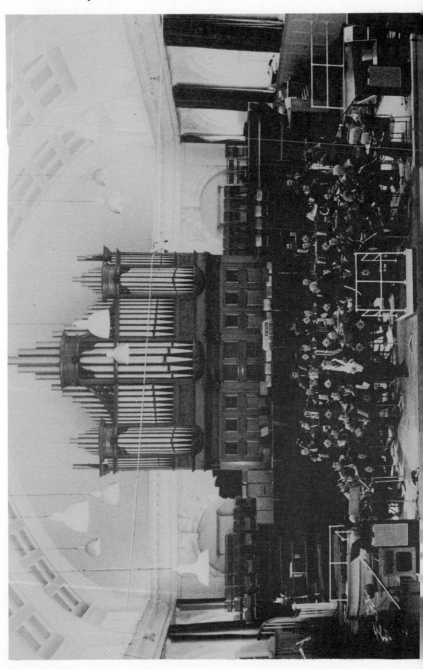

Tenor And Orchestra Or Wind Band

ABSIL, Jean: Berceuse (McGinnis & Marx)
BORSCHEL, E: Kubanisches Liebeslied (Frolich)
BUSCHMANN, R: Tenor Talen (Breitkopf)
DUCKWORTH, W: Fragments (Seesaw)
GLASER, W: Concerto (Stims, Sweden)
HARTLEY, Walter: Concertino (Dorn)
HARVEY, Paul: Concertino (Maurer)
JOLAS, B: Points d'Or (Ricordi)
LACOUR, Guy: Pièce Concertante (Billaudot)
LANE, R: Suite (B & H)
MIHALOVICI, M: Chant Premier (Heugel)
SCHMIDT, W: Concerto (Western)
STEINBACHER, E: Pièces (Frolach)
SYMONDS, N: Autumn Nocturne (Canadian)
WEINZWEIG, J: Divertimento (Canadian)
WILDER, Alec: Concerto (Western)

Baritone And Orchestra or Wind Band

HARVEY, Paul: Concertino (Maurer). The three Concertinos for soprano, tenor and baritone are orchestrated for the same eleven instruments as the Ibert. The entire trilogy was premiered at the World Saxophone Congress in London in 1976 at the Royal College of Music, the soloists being The Composer (soprano), James Houlik (tenor) and David Lawrence (baritone).
RIEUNIER, JP: Volume 2 (Leduc)
SKROWACZEWSKI, S: Ricercari Notturni (European/American).

Solo Repertoire With Piano Accompaniment

A particularly useful and interesting series for all saxophones and piano has recently been started by the American publishers Roncorp, P.O. Box 724, Cherry Hill, NJ 08003, USA.

Opposite page
World Saxophone Congress, 1976. The Royal College of Music, London.
The author as soloist in the first performance of Gordon Jacob's '*Miscellanies*' for alto saxophone and Wind Band, with the Band of the Irish Guards

It is called The Adolphe Sax Series, and consists of reissues of several pieces which were written by composer friends of Adolphe Sax for a small publishing house which he owned and operated from the late 1850's until he went bankrupt in 1878. At the ensuing bankruptcy sale, the tin lithograph plates for 189 pieces were sold, consequently they have been out of print ever since.

Roncorps are now republishing the best of these; they were all written for the express purpose of showing off the new saxophone to the best advantage, so they are extremely effective material for contests and auditions.

In the following lists, I do not include details of the many transcriptions of Baroque flute and oboe sonatas, which are, nonetheless, extremely important repertoire for saxophonists nowadays, for examinations and recitals. The biggest collection of these is Leduc's series, *Les Classiques des Saxophones*, arranged by Marcel Mule and Jean-Marie Londeix, but there are very many others, from various publishers. I have included a few arrangements which are different from this body of Baroque material.

Soprano And Piano

BLAVET/WOLFE: Sonata (Roncorp)
BIZET/HARVEY: Spanish Serenade (Roncorp)
BONNARD, Alain: Sonata No. 1 (EFM)
CARAVAN, Ronald L: Sonata (Ethos)
CLÉRISSE, Robert: *A l'Ombre du Clocher* (Leduc)
COWLES, Colin: *Spree* (Studio)
FELD, Jindrich: Elégie, Sonata (Leduc)
HANMER, Ronald: Saxophone Samples (Studio)
HARVEY, Paul: Contest Solo No. 4 (Studio)
HEATH, David: *Out of the Cool* (Chester)
PRESSER, William: Arioso (Presser)
SINGELÉE, Jean Baptiste: Caprice, Op. 80 and Fantaisie, Op. 89, (Roncorp's Adolphe Sax Series).

Alto And Piano

ABSIL, Jean: Sonata, Fantaisie Caprice, Cinq Pièces Faciles (Lemoine)

AMELLER, André: Suite d'Après Rameau, Kesa, Jeux de Table, Baie-Comeau (Leduc)

AMOS, Keith: Compositae Alto Sax (CMA)

ARBAN, Joseph: Caprice et Variations (Roncorp's Adolphe Sax Series)

BEECKMAN, Nazaire: Deuxième Morceau de Concert (GB)

BIZET/HARVEY: Spanish Serenade (Roncorp)

BONNEAU, Paul: Deux Caprices, Pièce Concertante, Suite (Leduc)

BOZZA, Eugène: Many effective short pieces all published by Leduc.

BUMCKE, Gustave: Concert Waltz (Ben)

COWLES, Colin: Miniature Suite, Scherzino (Studio)

CRESTON, Paul: Sonata Op. 19 (Shawnee)

DAMASE, Jean-Michel: Vacances, Note à note, Azur (GB)

DANKWORTH, John: Domnerus (Cascade)

DENISOV, Ivan: Sonata (Leduc)

DESENCLOS, Alfred: Prelude, Cadence et Final (Leduc)

DUBOIS, Pierre-Max: Many effective short pieces mostly published by Leduc.

GEE, Harry R.: First and Second Ballades (Kendor)

GUILHAUD/VOXMAN: First Concertino (Rubank)

HARVEY, Paul: Contest Solo No. 2, *The Singing Saxophone*, Vols. 1 & 2 (Studio). Alto Saxophone Solos, Vols 1 & 2 (Chester/ Music Sales).

HEATH, David: Reflections (Studio)

HINDEMITH, Paul: Sonata (Schott)

JACOB, Gordon: Variations on a Dorian Theme (Emerson)

JOLIVET, André: Fantaisie Impromptu (Leduc)

MAURICE, Paule: *Tableaux de Provence* (Lemoine)

RIDOUT, Alan: Concertino (Emerson)

ROSSINI/HARVEY: Bologna Variations (Roncorp)

SAVARI, Jean-Nicholas: Fantaisie sur des Motifs du Freischütz. (Roncorp's Adolphe Sax Series)

83

TCHEREPNINE, Alexandre: Sonatine Sportive (Leduc)
TOMASI, Henri: Introduction et Danse, Chant Corse, Ballade (Leduc)
TUTHILL, Burnett: Sonata Op. 20 (Southern)
VAUGHAN WILLIAMS, Ralph: Six Studies in English Folksong (SB)
WILDER, Alec: Sonata (Margueritat)
WOODS, Phil: Sonata (Kendor)

Tenor And Piano

AMOS, Keith: Compositae Tenor Sax (CMA)
CLÉRISSE: Prélude et Divertissement (GB)
COWLES, Colin: Five for a Tenor, (Studio) Of Spain, Pastoral (Dorn), Recit and Air (Studio)
DEMERSSEMAN, Jules: Premier Solo Andante et Bolero (Roncorp's Adolphe Sax Series)
GUILHAUD/VOXMAN: First Concertino (Rubank)
HANMER, Ronald: Saxophone Samples (Studio)
HARVEY, Paul: Contest Solo No. 1, *The Singing Saxophone* Vols. 1 & 2 (Studio). Tenor Saxophone Solos Vols. 1 & 2 (Chester/ Music Sales).
IBERT, Jacques: *Mélopée (Lemoine)*
SINGELÉE, Jean Baptiste: Adagio et Rondo, Op. 63 (Roncorp's Adolphe Sax Series)
Solo de Concert Op. 83 (Rubank)
4th Solo de Concert (Molenaar)
STENT, Keith: Simply Sax (Fentone)
TUTHILL, Burnett: Sonata Op. 56 (Southern)

Baritone And Piano

COWLES, Colin: A Miniature Suite (Studio)
HARVEY, Paul: Contest Solo No. 5 (Studio)
SINGELÉE, Jean Baptiste: Septième Solo de Concert (Roncorp's Adolphe Sax Series).

Saxophone Duets

Duets are the most useful teaching aid for rhythm reading and
intonation. However, in my opinion, music publishers waste a
lot of time and money printing SAME PITCH saxophone duets.
There is just no need for them, because all oboe duets suit the
saxophone range exactly, as do the wealth of Baroque flute
duets, which rarely go above top F. I keep piles of flute duets in
my teaching cupboard, and use them constantly, much more
than duets published for same pitch saxophones. Particular
favourites are the many duets by François Devienne.

What the saxophone needs a lot more of is Eb/Bb duets; by far
the most effective and useful combination is alto and tenor. Here
is a list of duets not for same pitch saxophones. A recent trend is
to have a playing score in same pitch, and a separate 2nd part for
tenor. This is a very good idea if the ranges are suitable; I have
marked these 'AT or AA'.

BEEKUM, Jan Van: Duets for Saxophones (Harmonia) AT
COWLES, Colin: Mixed Doubles (Fentone) AT
HARVEY, Paul: Concert Duets (Roncorp), *Equal Partners* Vols. 1
& 2 (Cascade) AT. *Take Away For Two*: Cl & Alto Sax (Mayhew)
Six Duets on the works of Berr, Five More Duets on Berr
(Studio) AT.
JACOB, Gordon: Duo for Soprano and Alto Saxes (Emerson).
RAE, James: Jazzy Duets (Universal) AT or AA
STREET, Karen: Dizzy Duets (Emerson) AT or AA

USA Agents:

Studio Music: Musicians' Publications, PO box 7160, West
Trenton, NJ. 08628 Tel: (609) 882 8131 fax: (609) 882 3182.
Kevin Mayhew: Mel Bay Publ. Inc., Unit 4, Industrial Drive,
Pacific, MO. 6309-3611
Editions Maurer: M. Baron Co., PO box 149, Oyster Bay, NY.
11771
Clarinet Classics (for Mule and Wiedoeft CD's): Qualiton
Imports Ltd., 24-02, 40th. Ave., Long Island City, NY, 11101

Twelve
Methods, Studies and other Publications

Methods

BROWN, John Robert: *How to Play Saxophone* (Elm Tree Books)
BUMCKE: *Saxophone Schüle* (Benj)
DE VILLE: *Universal Method* (Fisc)
DORSEY: *Saxophone Method* (TPF)
HERFURTH: *A Tune a Day* (Bost)
KLOSÉ: *Méthode Complète* (Leduc)
LONDEIX, Jean-Marie: *Playing the Saxophone* (Lemoine)
RAE, James: *Introducing the Saxophone* (Universal)
RAVENSCROFT, Raphael: *The Complete Saxophone Player* (4 Vols.) (Music Sales)
ROUSSEAU, Eugene: *Method* (Kjos) and *Saxophone High Tones* (Étoile)
VOXMAN, Hymie: *Rubank Method* (3 Vols) (Rubank).
WASTALL, Peter: *Learn as you Play* (B & H)
WOLFE, George: *Preparatory Method for Saxophone* (Roncorp).

Scale Books

They are all entitled: 'Scales and Arpeggios'.
Edited by: DE SMET, Robin: (Fentone)
HARLE, John: (Universal)
SPARKE, Philip: (Studio)
WASTALL, Peter: (B & H)
Bear in mind that any OBOE scale book or study will be in exactly the right written range for the saxophone.

Studies

BEEKUM, Jan Van: *Animato*, 107 short technical studies, and *Super Saxophones*, 35 studies on scales and chords (Harmonia/Kalmus).

BOZZA: *12 Études Caprices* (Leduc).

BUMCKE: Many study books (Benj)

COWLES, Colin: *Finger Bobbins* (Studio)

DAVIES & HARRIS: 80 Graded Studies and *Improve Your Sight Reading* (Faber)

GEE, Harry R: *Progressive and Varied Etudes* (Southern)

HARLE, John: *Easy Classical Studies* (Universal).

HARVEY, Paul: *Saxophone Workbook* (Studio).

HOVEY, Nilo: *Practical Studies*, 2 Vols (Belwin).

JETTEL, Rudolf: Several Volumes of Studies (Doblinger).

KLOSÉ: *Daily Exercises* (Leduc).

LACOUR, Guy: *Études Faciles et Progressives* and many other excellent studies (Billaudot).

Guy Lacour, playing an E*b*
Contrabass saxophone by
Buffet-Crampon, at the 1976
World Saxophone Congress

LONDEIX, Jean-Marie: Many excellent studies (Leduc & Lemoine).

MULE, Marcel: The largest body of study material in the whole saxophone repertoire, all worthy of intensive practice (Leduc).

Orchestral Excerpts

RONKIN, Bruce and FRASCOTTI, Robert: *The Orchestral Saxophonist*, Vols 1 & 2. (Roncorp)

Specialist Altissimo Books

NASH, Ted: *Studies in High Harmonics* (MCA)
RASCHER, Sigurd: *Top Tones for the Saxophone* (Fisc)
ROUSSEAU, Eugene: *Saxophone High Tones* (Étoile)

Jazz Studies

Improvisation Methods
AEBERSOLD, Jamey: A whole series of books and play along records (Jazzwise).
MARSHALL, Art: *The Liveliest Way to Take up Jazz* (Chester/Music Sales).
Studies
HARVEY, Paul: *Jazz from the Beginning* (Fentone/De Haske)
Jazz Rhythms (Kevin Mayhew)
NIEHAUS, Lennie: *Basic Jazz Conception* 2 Vols., *Intermediate Jazz Conception, Advanced Jazz Conception, Developing Jazz Concepts, The Blues.* (Try Publ. Co. Obtainable in UK from Jazzwise).
RAE, James: *20 Modern Studies* (Universal). *Progressive Jazz Studies* (Faber). *Blue Saxophone* (Universal). *Jazz and Rock Saxophone* (Universal).

Specialist Saxophone Magazines

The Saxophone Journal: PO Box 206, Medfield, Massachusetts, 02052, USA.
Clarinet and Saxophone: (Journal of the Clarinet and Saxophone Society of Great Britain).
167 Ellerton Road, Tolworth, Surbiton, Surrey KT6 7UB.
The Saxophone Symposium: (Journal of the North American Saxophone Alliance), 2232 Bowie Drive, Carrollton, Texas 75006. USA.

Le Saxophone: (Journal de L'Association Des Saxophonistes de France).

Journal De L'association Internationale Pour L'essor Du Saxophone.

Boletín Informativo De La Asociación De Saxofonistas Españoles.

Books On The Saxophone

DAWSON, James: *Music for Saxophone by British Composers* (Dorn).

GEE, Harry R: *Saxophone Soloists and their Music* (Indiana).

HARVEY, Paul: *The Saxophonist's Bedside Book* (Fentone) and *Bandroom Jottings* (Egon).

HORWOOD, Wally: *Adolphe Sax, his life and legacy* (Egon).

KOCHNITZKY, Leon: *Sax and his Saxophone* (North American Saxophone Alliance).

KOOL, Jap: *Das Saxophon*: English translation by Lawrence Gwozdz (Egon).

LONDEIX, Jean-Marie: *125 ans de Musique pour Saxophone* (Leduc) and *Musique pour Saxophone* Volume 2 (Roncorp).

Jean-Marie Londeix

ROUSSEAU, Eugene: *Marcel Mule, his life and the saxophone* (Étoile).

TEAL, Larry: *The Art of Saxophone Playing* (Summy-Birchard).

I cannot leave the subject of books on the saxophone without mentioning my own favourite, which, unfortunately, has been out of print for many years. I found my copy among a pile of old music given to me by the son of a deceased saxophonist.

It is only a nineteen page booklet, but contains invaluable advice, vividly put over. The title is: *The Saxophone Embouchure*, but it deals with much more than that, being a whole guide to tone production. It was written in 1925 by WALTER M. EBY, who was also the author of a four part *Scientific Method for Saxophone*. Some of this is rather dated, but it contains much valuable practice material, so is also well worth looking out for in second hand shops and piles of old music.

Both were originally published by Walter Jacobs Inc., 799, Seventh Avenue, New York 19, USA. They were distributed in the UK by Robbins Music Corporation, Francis, Day and Hunter of 138 Charing Cross Road, and Scarth Ltd, 55 Charing Cross Road.

Thirteen
Influential Saxophonists

This is a very condensed list of the players, both jazz and straight, who have been, or are being, the most INFLUENTIAL in forming the ideas, styles and enthusiasms of young players who may hear them or study with them.

Needless to say, there are many fine players whom I have had to miss out, otherwise the entire book would have become a saxophonists' directory.

I come across amazing gaps in young people's knowledge; for instance a pupil purporting to be keen on jazz who had never heard of Coleman Hawkins! How can someone be a saxophone player in any style and not have heard of Mule and Rascher?

So this list is to fill a few of these gaps in a most rudimentary way, in the hope that students will go on to look for recordings of these great players, or read their writings and generally take an interest in what's going on, and what has gone before.

The Jazz Masters

BECHET, Sidney (soprano)
b. New Orleans, La 1897 d. Garches, France 1959.
Bechet was already a world famous jazz clarinettist before he took up the soprano saxophone. The early sopranos having very unpredictable intonation, he developed an extremely wide vibrato to counteract this, which eventually became his trademark.

CARNEY, Harry (baritone)
b. Boston, Mass, 1910. d. New York, 1974.
He started on piano and clarinet, joined Duke Ellington's Band in 1927, eventually to become an institution as the definitive baritone player.

CARTER, Benny (alto)
b. New York, 1907.
One of the most versatile jazzmen of all time. As well as being a fine composer and arranger (he was a staff arranger for the BBC in London for a time in the 30's) he also played excellent trumpet.

COLTRANE, John (tenor)
b. Hamlet NC 1926. d. Huntington NY 1967.
'Trane' started in the US Navy Band, worked with Miles Davis, and was active in the bebop scene for several years. From 1965 his playing became more avant garde, and he was instrumental in the increasing influence of modal scales on jazz.

DESMOND, Paul (alto)
b. San Francisco, Cal, 1924. d. New York 1977.
Inextricably linked to pianist Dave Brubeck, with whose quartet he made many recordings during the 50's and 60's, including the best known, *Take Five*.

DORSEY, Jimmy (alto)
b. Shenandoah, Pa, 1904. d. New York 1957.
A very popular bandleader of the 30's and 40's, brother of the famous trombonist Tommy Dorsey. His most famous composition *Oodles of Noodles*, is typical of his virtuoso solo style which owed much to the Rudy Wiedoeft tradition carried on into the jazz age.

FREEMAN, Bud (tenor)
b. Chicago, Ill. 1906.
Started on C melody; played with Ben Pollack, Ray Noble, Tommy Dorsey and Benny Goodman, and worked in Europe a good deal in the 60's and 70's.

92

GETZ, Stan (tenor)
b. Philadelphia, Pa, 1927. d. 1992.
Started his career with Stan Kenton, Benny Goodman and Woody Herman. Considered one of the most creative and melodic innovators of the tenor, he enjoyed great commercial success with the bossa nova movement.

HAWKINS, Coleman (tenor)
b. St Joseph, Mo, 1904. d. New York 1969.
A top swing tenor of the 30's, working with Fletcher Henderson and in Europe, Hawk's comprehension of difficult chord progressions helped him to adjust to the new styles of the 40's when he worked with Dizzy Gillespie and Thelonius Monk.

HODGES, Johnny (alto)
b. Cambridge, Mass 1906. d. New York 1970.
His alto sound was the most distinctive trademark of the Duke Ellington Band, with whom he played for over a quarter of a century, from 1928.

MULLIGAN, Gerry (baritone)
b. New York, 1927.
The most important baritone specialist since Harry Carney. He worked with many famous bands, but it was with his several Quartets that he achieved his greatest success.

NIEHAUS, Lennie (alto)
b. St Louis, Miss. 1929.
The saxophone's greatest jazz educator, author of the 'Jazz Conception' series. He was a member of the Stan Kenton Band, and an active session player and arranger in Hollywood. He was music supervisor for *Bird*, Clint Eastwood's film about:

PARKER, Charlie (alto)
b. Kansas City, Miss 1920. d. New York 1955.
One of the greatest innovators in the history of jazz, not just the saxophone. After an unpromising start in the business he became interested in advanced harmony, his studies in this field, coupled with unrelenting technical practice on the saxophone, leading to his pioneering the bebop style in the mid 1940's.

93

PEPPER, Art (alto)
b. Gardena, Cal. 1925. d. Los Angeles, Cal. 1982.
Working with Stan Kenton and Buddy Rich, he developed a distinctive, lyrical style. His personal life, however, was a tragedy of drug dependence and imprisonment.

ROLLINI, Adrian (bass sax)
b. New York, 1904. d. Homestead, FLA. 1956.
The only bass saxophone specialist to come to prominence as a jazz soloist. He worked in London in the late 20's and early 30's.

ROLLINS, Sonny (tenor)
b. New York, 1929.
Working with Coltrane in New York in the late 40's he transferred the Parker tradition to the tenor, using his own style.

TRUMBAUER, Frankie (C Melody)
Although first known as a C melody soloist, he later played alto, working with many famous bands and leading his own. In one of these, in St Louis, his trumpet player was Bix Beiderbecke.

WOODS, Phil (alto)
b. Springfield, Mass. 1931.
Worked with Dizzy Gillespie, Thad Jones and Benny Goodman in the 50's and 60's. He has lived in Europe and California, and now does a lot of teaching and writing on the East Coast.

YOUNG, Lester (tenor)
b. Woodville, Miss. 1907. d. New York 1959.
In his youth greatly influenced by Frankie Trumbauer, the C melody sound led him to develop a soft, light tone on the tenor. This approach laid the groundwork for bop and the modern cool sound.

A Selection Of Influential Straight Players And Teachers

ABATO, Vincent
b. Willmerding, Penn. 1920.
For many years bass clarinet and saxophone player at the
Metropolitan Opera in New York. Made well known recordings
of Glazounov and Ibert.

ALLARD, Joseph
b. Lowell, Mass. 1910. d. 1991.
An active player and later a highly respected teacher at Juilliard
and New York University.

BECKENSTEIN, Raymond
b. Brooklyn NY. 1923.
Leader of the New York Saxophone Quartet for over thirty
years, and a top New York studio player.

BILGER, David
b. Reading Pa. 1945.
A leading recitalist and conductor of the Saxophone Sinfonia, he
is an authority on the saxophone mouthpiece, having produced
several of his own design.

BLACK, Robert
b. Sentinel, Okla, 1951.
Leader of the Chicago Saxophone Quartet and a Professor at
Roosevelt University. He is the founder of The Saxophone Shop
in Evanston, Ill.

BOGAARD, Ed
b. Weesp, Holland. 1943.
Professor at the Sweelinck Conservatory in Amsterdam, and
founder of the Netherlands Saxophone Quartet.

BRISCUSO, Joseph
b. St Louis, Miss. 1939.
Professor at Towson State University, Baltimore, and Director
of the American Single Reed Workshop.

BRODIE, Paul
b. Montreal, Canada 1934.
One of the founders of the World Saxophone Congress, in Chicago in 1969. He is Canada's most active saxophonist, touring all over the world, and has made a great many recordings. The first saxophonist to make a concert tour of China.

BRYMER, Jack
b. South Shields, 1915.
Although best known as Britain's leading clarinettist for many years, he has always played the saxophone as well, most notably from 1966, when he took over the leadership of the Michael Krein Quartet. He has also recorded the Coates Saxo-Rhapsody and played many orchestral saxophone parts with the London Symphony Orchestra.

CLINCH, Peter
b. Geraldton, Western Australia, 1930.
Senior Lecturer at Melbourne State University Conservatory and one of Australia's leading soloists, he is recognised as an expert in acoustics.

DANEELS, François
b. Tubize, Belgium, 1921.
Founder of the Quatuor Belge de Saxophones in 1953, and Professor at the Royal Conservatoire in Brussels from the following year.

DEFFAYET, Daniel
b. Paris, France, 1922.
Took over from Marcel Mule as Professor at the Paris Conservatoire in 1968. Has led his own Quartet since 1956, and does most of the saxophone work with the Berlin Philharmonic.

DELANGLE, Claude
b. Lyon, France, 1957.
In 1989, Deffayet retired from the post of Professor of Saxophone at the Paris Conservatoire, and Claude Delangle was, in due course, appointed as his successor.

DESLOGES, Jacques
b. Paris, France, 1934.
Professor at the Conservatoire in Versailles from 1975, and leader of the Quatuour de Saxophones Jacques Desloges.

GRADWELL, Christopher
b. Aberdeen, Scotland, 1941.
Founder of the London Saxophone Quartet (1969–85) and of the British Woodwind Workshop (1973–82). He has been a Professor at Trinity College of Music, and is now Director of the Versatile Music Company, an Orchestral Contracting Organisation.

HARLE, John
b. Newcastle, 1956.
He was the first young English saxophonist to go to Paris to study with Deffayet and to devote his career entirely to straight saxophone performance. He was leader of the Myrha Quartet, and is now a Professor at the Guildhall School of Music.

HARVEY, Paul
b. Sheffield, 1935.
Leader of the London Saxophone Quartet (1969–85) and now Senior Professor at the Royal Military School of Music, Kneller Hall. Author, composer and arranger.

HEMKE, Frederick
b. Milwaukee, Wis. 1935.
Professor at Northwestern University, in Chicago, since 1963.

HOULIK, James
b. Bay Shore NY. 1942.
The leading straight tenor saxophone specialist. He teaches at North Carolina School of the Arts.

KREIN, Michael
1908–1966 (English).
He gave Britain its first saxophone quartet; the Krein Quartet was a popular broadcasting group during the 40's and 50's, playing mainly his own arrangements of light music.

97

James Houlik

LACOUR, Guy
b. Soissons, France. 1932.
Tenor saxophone specialist and composer, Director of the École Municipale de Musique at Mantes-la-Ville. He is particularly well known for his excellent books of studies.

LEAR, Walter
1894–1981 (English).
An orchestral bass clarinettist and saxophonist, he was a member of the BBC Symphony Orchestra for 23 years and of the Royal Philharmonic Orchestra for 20. He was Professor of Saxophone at Trinity College of Music for 50 years, and at the Royal Military School of Music, Kneller Hall, during the 1930's.

LEESON, Cecil
b. Candon, N. Dakota, 1902. d. 1989 Muncie, Ind.
Pioneer saxophone soloist; gave first performance of the Glazounov Concerto in the USA, taught at Northwestern and Ball State Universities.

LONDEIX, Jean-Marie
b. Libourne, France 1932.
Professor at the Bordeaux Conservatoire since 1970. Author of many educational books on the saxophone and arranger of much published material. In 1972 he founded the Association des Saxophonistes de Frances (AS. SA. FRA.).

MAUK, Steven
b. Greenville, Tenn. 1949.
Has taught at Ithaca College since 1975; he is noted for his soprano playing and his instructive articles on teaching.

MULE, Marcel
b. Aube, France, 1901.
Professor at the Paris Conservatoire from 1942–1968. The leading figure of the straight saxophone world, known affectionately as 'Le Patron'.

NODA, Ryo
b. Amagasaki, Japan 1948.
The first Japanese virtuoso to play extensively in the USA and Europe. He pioneered many avant-garde techniques, and has composed a number of works blending Japanese and Western styles.

RASCHER, Sigurd
b. Ebberfeld, Germany, 1907.
He was the first straight player to develop the altissimo register. In 1933 he left Germany to teach in Denmark and Sweden for five years, after which he went to the USA. The very many works written for Rascher include the Ibert Concertino, the Glazounov Concerto and the Coates Saxo-Rhapsody.

REGNI, Albert
b. Johnson City, NY. 1936.
The alto player in the New York Saxophone Quartet during the 1970's during which time he did most of the saxophone work with the New York Philharmonic. He later taught at the University of Texas.

99

ROUSSEAU, Eugene
b. Blue Island, Ill. 1932.
Chairman of the Woodwind Faculty at Indiana University, where he has taught since 1964. He is a greatly respected clinician, and the author of several educational publications, including the definitive book on the altissimo register.

SAKAGUCHI, Arata
b. Tokyo, Japan. 1910.
The father of the Japanese school of saxophone playing. Originally a cellist, he taught himself the saxophone from recordings and correspondence with Marcel Mule. Gave the first Japanese performances of all the main saxophone works and taught nearly every well known Japanese player.

SINTA, Donald
b. Detroit, Mich. 1937.
He succeeded Larry Teal as Professor at the University of Michigan in 1974.

TEAL, Larry
1905–1984.
A greatly respected pioneer of straight saxophone teaching in the USA, and was the first Professor of Saxophone to be appointed to a leading American University. (University of Michigan 1953).

THOMAS, Neville (Australia)
Professor of Saxophone at the Sydney Conservatorium, and founder of the Clarinet and Saxophone Society of New South Wales. Awarded Medal of the Order of Australia 1992.

TRIER, Stephen
b. Newbury, 1930.
Professor of Saxophone at the Royal College of Music, and bass clarinet/saxophone with the London Philharmonic Orchestra. He translated Londeix's *Playing the Saxophone* into English.

Finally, four influential players who cannot be classified as either jazz or straight, but who must be considered in any overall survey of the development of saxophone playing.

GALLODORO, Alfred (Al)
b. Birmingham, Alabama c. 1912.
One of the greatest doublers of all time; a phenomenal virtuoso on saxophone, clarinet and, notably, bass clarinet. He was a featured soloist with the Paul Whiteman Orchestra, and a Studio Player in New York, mostly with ABC. He was a fluent improviser in both the swing style and the older variation style, using double and triple tonguing to rival that of Rudy Wiedoeft.

GARDNER, Freddy
1911–1950 (English).
A brilliant instrumentalist associated with the Ray Noble and later Peter Yorke Orchestras. He had a very sweet sound, a wide vibrato and a good altissimo range.

GUREWICH, Jascha
1896–1938.
Born in Russia, he emigrated to the USA and was solo saxophonist with the Sousa Band. He wrote many brilliant light solos.

WIEDOEFT, Rudy
b. Detroit, Mich. 1893. d. Queens, NY 1940.
We looked at the influence of Wiedoeft's short, brilliant career in the history chapter. His many compositions are eagerly sought after by enthusiasts, and, hopefully, one day, may all be republished.

Fourteen
Discography

This selection of recordings has been made on the basis of which would be most instructive for a young player. In the case of solo albums I have chosen mostly those which include one or more works from the various examination syllabuses. With Quartets I have looked for the kinds of works a young quartet might be rehearsing, and works which could be used to demonstrate the possibilities of the medium to an interested composer.

In Britain there are quite a lot of specialist jazz record shops, so the numerous recordings of the influential jazz players listed in the previous chapter, and the many impressive jazz saxophonists recording today are readily available. Straight saxophone recordings, however, are notoriously difficult to find, or even to order from British record shops. It is therefore easier, and often quicker, to send to America for them, one of the best sources being:

Woodwind Service Inc. Box 206, Medfield Massachusetts, 02052.

There is no longer any hassle with currency exchange; nowadays you can pay by just giving a credit card number.

ABATO, Vincent : Ibert Concertino (Urania US 5146)
BANASZAK, Greg : Glazounov Concerto (Banaszak 001)
BERLINER QUARTET : Glazounov and Françaix
(Schwann VMS 1066)
BILGER, David : Milhaud Scaramouche (Trutone 520458)
BLACK, Robert : Concert Repertoire for Saxophone
(Ibert and Husa)

BORIOLI, Orazio : Grovlez Sarabande and Allegro. Ibert *Histoires* (Gallo-CD-516)

BORNKAMP, Arno : Creston, Hindemith and Denisov Sonatas (Globe 5032)

BRISCUSO, Joseph : Myres Sonatine. (Golden Crest. RE 7086).

BRODIE, Paul : Hindemith Sonata (Golden Crest RE 7056) Baroque Soprano (Golden Crest RE 7041) Sopranino and Soprano (Golden Crest RE 7049) The Golden Age of Saxophone (CBC. MVC 1005).

BRODIE QUARTET : Pierné Variations and Harvey *Robert Burns Suite*. (Golden Crest CRSQ 4154).

BRYMER, Jack : Coates, *Saxo-Rhapsody*. (CFPD 4456).

CHICAGO QUARTET : Rivier *Grave and Presto; Quartets by Barab and Karlins. (Mastersound DFCD1 – 014)*

DANEELS, François : (with the Belgian Radio Orchestra) Saxophone en Concert. Villa-Lobos *Fantaisie* and Harvey *Soprano Concertino*. (Zephyr Z23)

DANOVITCH QUARTET : Dubois Quartet (McGill 85022) Françaix Quartet (CBC MVC 1018)

DESLOGES, Jacques : Music of Paul Arma (Gasparo G5-214)

ENGLISH SAXOPHONE QUARTET : Glazounov, Pascal and Dubois Quartets (ESQ C5 103)

THE FAIRER SAX : Harvey *Robert Burns Suite*. (Saydisc CD-SLD 3)

GENEVA QUARTET : Pierné Variations, Rivier Grave et Presto, Dubois Quartet. (Gallo 30-495)

HARLE, John : Woods and Bennett Sonatas, Heath *Rumania*. (Hyperion CDA 66246)

Music of Dominic Muldowney (EMI 7497452)

Works by: Bennett, Debussy, Glazounov, Ibert, Villa Lobos, Muldowney and Heath (EMI Classics)

Works by: Bennett, Bryars, Myers, Nyman and Westbrook (ARGO).

HAYSTED, Ian : Harvey *Cool Music Series* (Fentone/De Haske Music)

Harvey *Contest Solos* (Studio Music)

Video: *Learn how to create ACOUSTIC EFFECTS on saxophone*. www.reedimensions.com

JORDAN, Bruce : Dubois Concertstück, Creston Concerto (Coronet LPS3103)

KLOCK, Lynn : Ibert Concertino, Glazounov Concerto (Open Loop Records 006)

Maurice *Tableaux de Provence*, Creston Sonata (Open Loop 007)

KYNASTON, Trent : Ingolf Dahl Concerto (Mark MC 1418)

Denisov and Heiden Sonatas (Coronet LPS3044)

Creston Sonata (SMR 19831)

LOS ANGELES QUARTET : Bach, *The Art of Fugue*. (Protone PR143/4)

LONDEIX, Jean-Marie : Hindemith and Denisov Sonatas (SNE 517)

Koechlin Études (Golden Crest 7098)

LONDON SAXOPHONE QUARTET : Jacob No. 1, Harvey, Cordell, Dubois, Absil (Roncorp EMS 020)

From Medieval to Jazz (Argo ZK 79)

The LSQ in Digital (Polyphonic PRCD 301)

MARSALIS, Branford : With the English Chamber Orchestra. Romances for Saxophone (CBS M42122)

MULE, Marcel: *Marcel Mule – Le Patron of the Saxophone.* (CC0013) and: *Marcel Mule – Le Patron of the Saxophone... Encore!* (CC0021). A wonderful collection of the master's solo and quartet recordings, brought to life by modern technology. Obtainable from: Clarinet Classics, 77 St. Albans Avenue, London E6 4HH. Tel/fax: +44 0208 472 2057.

NETHERLANDS QUARTET : Pierné, Françaix and Rivier (Nonsuch H71402)

NEW YORK QUARTET : Woods Three Improvisations (Stash STC015)

NOVA QUARTET : Paul Pierné *Trois Conversations* (Crystal S153)

Barab Quartet (MHS 912051K)

PHOENIX QUARTET : The Return of Bulgy Gogo; Carey Blyton Miniatures (Upbeat URCD 106)

PITTEL, Harvey : Maurice *Tableaux de Provence* (Crystal S105)

Creston Sonata (Crystal S157)

PITTEL QUARTET : Glazounov, Bozza 'Nuages' (Crystal S155)

POTTS, Leo : Maurice *Tableaux de Provence* (Crystal S159)

PRISM QUARTET : Singelée Premier Quatuor (Koch 70242)

RAHBARI, Sohre : Milhaud *Scaramouche*, Glazounov Concerto, Debussy Rhapsody, Ibert Concertino (Marco Polo 8.223374)

RAMSAY, Neal : Bonneau Caprice, Debussy 'Syrinx'

Maurice *Tableaux de Provence*, Woods Sonata, Creston Sonata.

(Cumberland CRP 8811)

RIJNMOND QUARTET : Desenclos Quartet, Bozza Andante & Scherzo (BV Haast 8804)

ROUSSEAU, Eugene : Jolivet Fantaisie-Impromptu (Coronet 1703)

Debussy Rhapsody, Villa-Lobos Fantasia (Delos D/CD 1007)

ROUSSEAU QUARTET : Linn Quartet (Golden Crest CRS 4224)

SAVIJOKI, Pekka : The French Saxophone (Bis 209)

SAXPAK : Light Septet Arrangements by Ted White. (M.W. Instruments Ltd, 11 Queens Parade, Ealing, London W5 3HU)

SAXTET : Montage (KGRS 1231)

SINTA, Donald : Creston Concerto (Golden Crest CRS 4211)

SONORA QUARTET : *Treasures*. Jean-Jean Quatuor. Harvey *Celtic Collage*. (Sonora Productions SQ 1190)

TEXAS QUARTET : *Something Completely Different* (TSQ-1)

Our First Nowell (TSQ)

VAN OOSTROM, Leo : *Licks and Brains* for Bass Saxophone (CVCD 13)

UNDERWOOD, Dale : Bozza Aria (Golden Crest RE 7101)

Heiden Sonata (Golden Crest 7067)

Eccles Sonata (Open Loop 009)

VERSAILLES QUARTET : Rivier *Grave et Presto* (Thesis 82052)

WATTERS, Mark : Baritone Saxophone Album (Crystal S152)

WIEDOEFT, Rudy : *Rudy Wiedoeft – Kreisler of the Saxophone*. (CC0018) At last we can hear a modern reproduction of the most legendary saxophonist of them all! Obtainable from:

Clarinet Classics, 77 St. Albans Avenue, London E6 4HH.

WYTKO, Joseph and WYTKO QUARTET : Creston Sonata and 2 Karlins Quartets. (CM 20012-12)

YOUNG, Keith : The Saxophone Music of Charles Koechlin. (Open Loop Records).

Fifteen
Glossary of French Technical Terms

A knowledge of French is vital to the serious student of the saxophone. The greater part of the literature on the instrument and commentaries on its repertoire are written in that language.

Yet even those with a fair command of everyday French could well be stumped by some of the terms for parts of the instrument which would not be found in a normal dictionary.

English professional saxophonists have always made trips to Paris to test and purchase instruments. With the advent of the Common Market and the opening of the Channel Tunnel this interchange should become even more frequent. This is a very basic vocabulary to which a travelling saxophonist could add from his or her own experience.

l'accord (m) – intonation, tuning
l'anche (f) – reed
   la coupe-anche – reed cutter
   la force – strength
   forte – hard
   faible/facile – soft
   moyenne – medium
   le roseau – cane
l'atelier (m) – workshop
le bec – mouthpiece
   la table – lay
   l'ouverture (f) – (tip) opening
   courte/longue – short/long (lay)
bas – flat (intonation)
le bocal – crook

le cordon – sling
la cordelière – sling
la clétage – keywork
le couvre-bec – mouthpiece cap
la culasse – bow (bottom of bell)
le doigté – fingering
l'écouvillon (m) – swab, pull-through
l'étui (m) – case
   la housse – case cover
haut – sharp (intonation)
la justesse – intonation, tuning, accuracy
le liège – cork
le pavillon – bell
la perce – bore
le pilier – pillar (post)
le plateau – finger plate (pearl)
le protège-bec – mouthpiece cushion, patch
le ressort – spring
le rouleau – roller
le suraigu – altissimo (register)
le tampon – pad
la touche (or clé) – key
la vis – screw
   la vis charnière – rod
   la vis pointue – point screw

Notes:		
do or ut –	C
ré –	D
mi –	E
fa –	F
sol –	G
la –	A
si –	B
bémol –	flat ($\flat$)
dièse –	sharp (#)
bécarre –	natural ($\natural$)

French is so much the language of the saxophone that it is often used as a 'lingua franca' between saxophonists of different nationalities.

Here is a little reminiscence to illustrate this, entitled:
The Night I Invented Frapanese.

I was having a convivial meeting in Hiroshima with Keiji Ueda, the Professor of Saxophone at the local university. Although he spoke some English he found it rather hard going, and my Japanese was limited to ordering beer, so we conversed in French, in which he was fluent, having studied with Jean-Marie Londeix in Bordeaux.

When it was my turn to order some more beer I confidently declaimed to the waitress, 'Ni biru, onegaishimas'. She went to fetch the beers and we continued our in depth discussion of saxophone matters in French. The waitress returned and placed huge tankards of beer in front of us, at which point I intended to say 'Domo arigato' which is Japanese for 'Thank you very much'. Instead I was horrified to hear, issuing from my lips, the bizarre Frapanese expression: 'MERCI ARIGATO'. Keiji collapsed in hysterics, and the waitress merely bowed, giving me the patient smile which the Japanese reserve for eccentric foreigners!

Sixteen
Some Unusual Saxophones

The Conn-O-Sax

The basic design of the ordinary, workaday saxophone has hardly changed at all since Adolphe Sax's time, but some quite exotic forms of the family have come and gone over the years. The heyday for these was the 1920's, when the enormous volume of saxophone sales enabled the American manufacturers to experiment, in attempts to outdo one another with new 'novelty' instruments.

In those days, the C melody was the biggest seller, and the Conn Company of Elkhart, Indiana, decided to popularize another of Sax's original F – C family by producing a modern version of the F alto. They called it, however, the F Mezzo-soprano, because its bore dimensions were relatively closer to a soprano than to an alto, which was said to give it a tone combining the brilliance of the soprano with the sweetness of the alto.

To the uninitiated, however, it did not look all that different from the other saxophones, so they decided to produce an alternative form that would really be a novelty. This rejoiced in the evocative name of the Conn-O-Sax. It had a straight body, a slightly curved crook at the top, and, at the bottom, a bulb-shaped bell, similar to the larger members of the oboe family.

The straight-bodied shape has been used for saxophones as big as the Eb alto size, and the Conn-O-Sax must have been nearly as long as one of these, as it had a range down to bottom A, the lowest key being operated by the right thumb, not by the left thumb, as on a modern low A baritone. It also had keys up to a top G, which was operated by the first finger of the right hand.

Playing cor anglais and horn in F parts would have been an obvious use for it. Conn produced an elaborate advertisement with the slogan: 'Plays like saxophone; sounds like English horn; looks like Heckelphone.'

The story of these instruments has a very sad ending. They barely survived into the 1930's, as the popularity of saxophone groups touring the vaudeville circuit died out with the end of the 20's. The unsold Mezzo-sopranos and Conn-O-Saxes were relegated to Conn's Instrument Repairing School in Elkhart, where they served as guinea pigs for apprentice repairmen up to the 1940's.

The 'One Hand' Saxophone

The Conn Company was also responsible for the most bizarre saxophone design of all, again in the F mezzo-soprano range. This was an ingenious layout of keywork with seven pearls and all the other keys on the lower half of the body, so that the entire range could be played with the right hand only.

Very little is known about this right hand saxophone, but the one existing example has been very well photographed and documented by the noted collector, Theodore McDowell of Stokie, Illinois.

It was very likely a one off special order, as there is no serial number on the instrument. Its purpose may have been for a vaudeville performer to play duets with himself. Credence is lent to this theory by the still existing original double case, which has another space shaped like a cornet.

I myself remember playing in a variety theatre in the late 1940's, accompanying an 'act' who played duets with himself on soprano and alto. I think he played the alto with his left hand and the soprano with his right hand on the top half of the body. It was a straight bodied soprano; I remember thinking that a curved soprano would have made things easier. A 'right handed' F mezzo-soprano would have been even better, but the mind boggles at producing a cornet embouchure with the other side of the mouth!

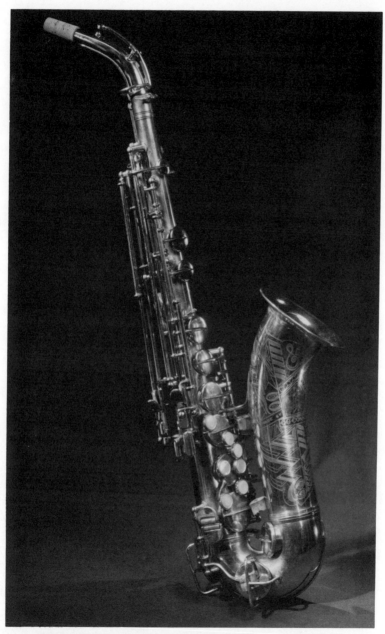

The unique 'right hand only' Conn mezzo-soprano saxophone in F.
(Photograph by courtesy of Theodore McDowell and Wally Horwood)

The Loomis 'Double Resonance' Alto

It is frustrating to learn that two of the saxophone's worst problems, the compromise placing of the two octave vents and the necessity of sliding on both sets of little finger keys, were being solved as long ago as 1913 and the improvements were actually patented in 1920.

Allen Loomis (1877–1948) was chief research engineer of the Conn Company from 1927, but designed this revolutionary saxophone while working in the car industry. The name 'Double Resonance' refers to the fact that at least two tone holes are always open below the one from which a note is coming. This eliminates the slightly veiled effect which can result from cross fingering on the conventional instrument.

The theoretically acoustically perfect saxophone would have a separate octave vent for every note in the second register, so our conventional two vents must have a large element of compromise. Loomis increased the number of octave vents to three on his double resonance model and added a fourth while working for Conn in the 30's. These were all fully automatic, opening separately from one octave key.

The Loomis alto had a range down to bottom A, but its most interesting innovation was the possibility of alternative fingerings for the two little fingers, putting the saxophone's bottom notes at last on a par with the comparative sophistication of the Boehm system clarinet.

There was a right C# key and a left Eb key, so that many of the awkward sliding intervals on a conventional saxophone, such as Bb to Db, B to C# and C to Eb could be played L–R or R–L. This, to my mind, would have been one of the most useful improvements which could have been made to standard saxophone mechanism.

Yet only six of these instruments were ever made, and none of the big firms, not even Conn, ever considered tooling up to put them into commercial production. Why was this?

We can guess the reason quite easily. The period 1915 to 1929 was the zenith of saxophone production in the USA, when over a million saxophones were manufactured and sold. The makers

Evette & Schaeffer "Apogée" System Saxophones.

The latest perfection in Saxophones is demonstrated by this new system, "The Apogée" Buffet make and built upon the famous system of Evette & Schaeffer, Paris.

Saxophone players should not fail to look into the merits of these very latest improvements, as they combine a number of exceptional qualities entirely lacking in even the best productions of the past.

Among the most noticeable improvements and additions to the "Apogée" Saxophones we will mention the following :

(1) A new patent double key for the production of B. for the little finger of the right hand only.

(2) A new patent double key for the production of G sharp for either the first or second finger of the right hand.

(3) A new patent double key for the production of D. for the first finger of the right hand.

(4) A new patent mechanism permitting the production of B flat, B and C sharp with the little finger of the left hand alone.

The principal advantages which these new Apogée Saxophones offer as compared with the older instruments are that successive intervals such as :

Bb, B♯   Bb, Eb   B♮, C♯   B♭, Eb

B♮, G♯   C♯, Eb

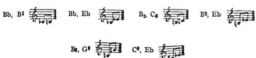

as well as the Chromatic Scale can be executed very easily, owing to the fact that the interval B. may be produced with equal ease, with the little finger of either the right or left hand, and the intervals Bb   and C♯   with the little finger of left hand only.

In conclusion we mention the ease with which a trill may be executed on either of these G♯: with the first finger of the right hand, and the ease and evenness with which such passages as the following: may be produced with the first finger of the right hand by means of the double key D.

A page from the 1908 Carl Fischer instrumental catalogue, illustrating the innovative key mechanisms found on the Evette-Schaeffer saxophones. Most of these were copied by Holton for use on their saxophones before and after the Wiedoeft models.

113

could sell as many instruments as they could produce, so if people were so eager to buy existing models, why should they spend a great deal of money setting up a production line for a much more complicated model which would have to retail at anything up to twice as much as an ordinary saxophone, with the attendant risk that the public would not wish to pay so much more for its added sophistication.

In spite of this disappointment, Loomis went on to have a successful career with the Conn Company and in 1942 was co-inventor of the first stroboscopic tuner.

The Grafton Acrylic Saxophone

As we have already remarked, the saxophone does not have to be made of metal. Wood, although possible, is highly impractical, but what about today's most popular alternative material, some form of plastic?

The saxophone has changed less since its invention than any other woodwind instrument; the Grafton was really the only totally innovative concept of saxophone design, and the only successful attempt to make a saxophone in a non-metallic material.

It took its name from Grafton Way, off Tottenham Court Road, where its inventor, Hector Sommaruga, had his first London workshop in 1942. Born in Milan in 1904, Ettore, to give him his real Italian Christian name, went to Paris in 1922 to work in the instrument making trade. In 1926 he was sent to London to gold-plate saxophones for Hawkes & Son and to train their apprentices in the operation. After working again in Paris and then in Portugal, he settled permanently in England in 1936.

The creation of the Grafton suggests some interesting historical parallels; its patent was filed in 1945, almost a century after Adolphe Sax's original patent. Just as the great saxophone craze of the 1920's was to some extent produced by the euphoria following the end of the First World War, so the Grafton was very much a child of the end of the Second World War.

Plastics were a symbol of the new technology, having been developed extensively for various arms manufacturing purposes during the war. ICI produced the powder which was used by the

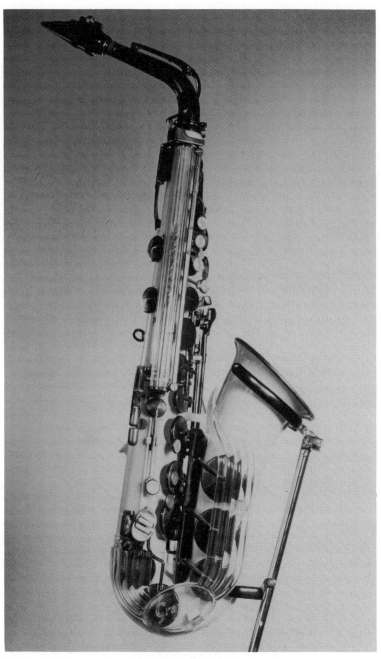

Grafton Acrylic alto
(John Sands' Collection)

engineering firm De La Rue to make the body, which was the largest piece of injection moulding attempted up to that time.

In 1946 an unplayable prototype, adorned with the slogan 'Built for Better Times Ahead' was displayed at a morale-boosting exhibition called 'Britain Can Make It'. One is tempted to comment that this was perhaps the only occasion in its entire existence when the saxophone has been a Politically Correct artifact!

The Grafton was eventually launched for public sale in 1950, enthusiastically endorsed by many top players of the day, including John Dankworth and Freddy Gardner. Its unusual appearance made an immediate impact; the white plastic body with gold lacquered keywork and crook and the clear plastic key guards were a completely new image. Being plastic, the walls of the body were thicker than metal would have to be, giving the instrument a generally fatter appearance and feel. Think how thin a metal clarinet looks compared to a wooden or plastic one. The mechanism, however, had a lighter feel, as needle springs could not be used, and piano wire springing took its place, which some players found to lack enough resistance for a clean, firm finger technique.

This may have been one of the reasons for its commercial failure; one is surprised, on checking dates, to find that production officially ceased in 1954. It seems amazing that such a well designed instrument, which had been so well advertised, selling at half the price of a comparable metal saxophone, should have only been manufactured for four years!

Other reasons often conjectured at are the danger of the body cracking if dropped; unwillingness of repairers to adjust the unusual springing; prejudice of teachers and some players, and the impossibility of having a matched section of Graftons. Don't forget, this was the heyday of the five sax Dance Band section, but only alto Graftons were ever made, as the injection moulding process could not cope with anything bigger at that time.

There are still quite a few Graftons about, and if you ever get a chance to try one, note what is possibly the most interesting fact about them. They sound very much the same as a metal saxophone, similar variations in timbre being produced by different mouthpieces. This goes to prove, yet again, that tone quality depends on the shape of the air column inside the instrument's body, rather than on the material of which it is made.

The Right Hand Articulated C# Mechanism (1984) designed by James Rae

The inspiration behind this device came from an awkward passage in the slow movement of the Dubois saxophone quartet. Here the Alto sax was required to play the following:-

The use of rollers made this possible but very cumbersome. James Rae thought that by adding an articulated C# key to the right hand little finger key cluster (as on the oboe) this would alleviate the situation. It not only did this but it also made the following much easier:-

The mechanism also enabled C# to be playable by the left hand little finger without the right hand C key, thus making C# to D# very easy. It almost eliminates the use of rollers.

He was so convinced that it was going to work that he fitted a very crude prototype to his Selmer Mk. VI alto. When he discovered that it was very successful, he approached Bill Wrathel who agreed to build a much more refined version. He did a first class job and James Rae has used it professionally ever since.

Right hand articulated C# mechanism
Designed by James Rae and built by Bill Wrathel

Seventeen
The Saxophone Today

There are two important facts about the saxophone today; more young people are studying the instrument seriously than ever before, and more composers are writing for it.

In Great Britain much of the credit for generating new repertoire must be given to John Harle, who is the first English player to have made a highly successful career purely as a saxophone soloist. His energy and high profile with the musical public have given rise to new works for the saxophone by Richard Rodney Bennett, Luciano Berio, Dominic Muldowney, Ned Rorem, Michael Berkeley, Michael Nyman, Gavin Bryars, David Heath, Mike Westbrook, Stanley Myers, Harrison Birtwistle, Wilfred Josephs and Phillip Glass.

John Harle
Britain's leading
saxophone soloist

119

There are also more active Saxophone Quartets in Britain than ever before, including the Apollo, Delta, English, Fairer Sax (now reduced to a trio, I understand), Northern, Phoenix, Saxology, Saxtet, and Scottish Quartets.

Never before have there been so many opportunities to study the saxophone seriously, with all the leading music colleges offering places for first study saxophonists, as shown by the following list of who is teaching where.

Professors of Saxophone at the Principal Colleges of Music in Britain

BIRMINGHAM CONSERVATOIRE: Andrew Tweed & Chris Gumbley

COLCHESTER INSTITUTE: Angela Fussell, Melanie Bush & Mike Hall

GUILDHALL SCHOOL OF MUSIC & DRAMA: Glenn Martin, Simon Haram, David Road, Jean Toussaint & Martin Hathaway

LEEDS COLLEGE OF MUSIC: Richard Ingham, Phil Chapman & Al Wood (Wind Co-ordinator)

LONDON COLLEGE OF MUSIC: Jimmy Hastings & Glenn Martin

ROYAL ACADEMY OF MUSIC: Richard Addison

ROYAL COLLEGE OF MUSIC: Kyle Horch & Martin Robertson

ROYAL MILITARY SCHOOL OF MUSIC, Kneller Hall: Frank Slack & Ian Haysted

ROYAL NORTHERN COLLEGE OF MUSIC: Rob Buckland & Mike Hall

ROYAL SCOTTISH ACADEMY OF MUSIC & DRAMA: Robert Fairley, Josef Pacewicz & Bobby Wishart

TRINITY COLLEGE OF MUSIC: Gerard McChrystal & Stan Sulzman

WELSH COLLEGE OF MUSIC & DRAMA: Gerard McChrystal, John Cooper & Peter Fielding

The Saxophone And Synthesiser Technology

Many people are confused as to the purpose of the various types of electronic wind instruments or 'wind synthesisers'. They are in no way intended to be substitutes for real woodwind instruments; if you want the sound of a saxophone, a clarinet or a flute, then the genuine articles are at hand, with no need to complicate them electronically.

What the wind synthesiser aims to do is to combine the best of two worlds; the woodwind instrument and the keyboard, linking the woodwind player's technique, phrasing and expression to keyboard possibilities such as chords, parallel intervals and a much wider pitch range.

The wind synthesiser on its own makes no sound, but has to be plugged into a tone generator, the quality of which is the most important factor in the success of these new techniques. The concept has been around for over twenty years, but the first widely used wind synthesiser, the Lyricon, was not a success because it predated the development of a communication device called MIDI.

Musical Instrument Digital Interface is the sound generating system which has been the catalyst in transforming the wind synthesiser from an interesting toy into a means of enhancing the range of possibilities available to the serious musician. The main quality of MIDI which has made such a difference is its ability to link together a large number of instruments, which can then be controlled from one source.

Several different models of wind synthesiser which can be linked to the MIDI system are on the market. The fingering is basically similar to a saxophone, but has five octave buttons, producing a range of nearly seven octaves. Some of the keys which raise a note a semitone, act on all notes, which gives many new fingering possibilities.

There is a beak mouthpiece, with a permanently attached plastic reed. This makes no sound on its own, but monitors the player's tonguing and embouchure inflections, such as vibrato

121

and pitch bends. Besides the chords, parallel intervals and large range already mentioned, accurate quarter tones are another possibility. There is also a hold button to sustain one note while playing others, and transposing buttons which automatically pitch the instrument in low or high C, Eb or Bb.

To hear effective use of wind synthesiser techniques in jazz, listen to several albums by Mike Brecker and Sal Gallina. In the straight field, new works for this medium have been written in the USA for Fred Hemke, John Sampen and Bruce Ronkin, and in the UK, for Richard Ingham and Peter Nichols, who has recently recorded 'Comics' by John Kefala Kerr, a work which creates multi-layered voices, coupled with the use of digital reverb, producing startling contrapuntal effects, all from one player.

Peter Nichols also told me of an excellent educational use for his wind synthesiser. At the Northern Saxophone Quartet jazz workshops he uses it as a bass voice, changing from string bass to bass guitar at the touch of a button, and in conjunction with a drum machine, providing an instant rhythm section.

But all this is by no means the end. At the time of writing, the latest thing is the SYNTHOPHONE. This is an actual saxophone, in fact a real Yamaha 23; packed with electronics in the crook, body and bell, which is closed off with a metal plate. Like other wind synthesisers, the synthophone cannot be played on its own as an acoustic saxophone, but when connected from a socket at the bottom of the bell, to a MIDI tone generator, it can be played with conventional saxophone technique. Its range is just over four octaves, and it has all the other wind synthesiser possibilities previously mentioned.

Many other amazing inventions will no doubt be following hard on the heels of the synthophone. Young players should bear in mind that the way forward is in creating new sounds, not imitating conventional instruments.

I propose a motto for all saxophonists of the future as they explore these wonderful developments:

'WE HAVE THE TECHNOLOGY, BUT DON'T FORGET THE MUSIC!'

The Saxophone In Pop Music

However you define the various styles of pop music; rock and roll, rhythm and blues, funk, punk, soul etc, the saxophone is often featured in the instrumental line up. There is no easily definable line where jazz is divided from pop, as many fine jazz players have enjoyed commercial success with pop groups, notably Phil Woods with Billy Joel and Branford Marsalis with Sting.

The pop style of saxophone playing is often traced back as far as Chu Berry, and, in the 40's, to Louis Jordan, but the style was really developed recognizably in the 50's, by such players as King Curtis, Sam Taylor and Lee Allen. Over the next couple of decades the players most identified with more recent trends in Afro-American pop music have been David Sanborn, Michael Brecker, Maceo Parker, Clarence Clemmons and Junior Walker, bringing us up to the present day with the very successful Kenny G.

Styles of contemporary pop music are very difficult to define precisely; some personal experience I have had of this has been playing bass clarinet for recordings and videos of Michael Kamen's two 'Rock Concertos', the first written for David Sanborn on alto sax and the second for the electric guitar of Eric Clapton.

Stylistically speaking, the 'Concerto for Sanborn' seemed to me to have its roots more in the Eric Coates Saxo-Rhapsody than in jazz or rock. It was mainly David Sanborn's tone, articulation and inflexions which gave the work its rock character. If it had been played on a straight mouthpiece, exactly as written, by a player such as the late Walter Lear, who was possibly the straightest of all saxophonists, then the work would have taken on the character of a 'middle of the road' rhapsodic concerto. To my mind, this demonstrates the saxophone's amazing ability to transform the style of any music which it plays, just by the use of a different mouthpiece and articulating differently. This is why we must be so careful to play baroque and classical transcriptions on appropriate equipment!

No standard line up of saxophones, comparable to the 2 alto, 2 tenor and baritone section of the Big Band, has ever become the norm in pop groups. Mostly the saxophone, usually tenor or alto, is used as a solo instrument, interpolating fills and responses to the lead singer. Sometimes one or more saxophones are used in combination with brass instruments, and a pop convention has grown up to call this a 'horn section', which is confusing in not distinguishing saxophones from trumpets and trombones.

The distinctively strident tone has developed of necessity in competition with the volume produced by electric guitars. Obviously a very wide lay mouthpiece is used, and a large proportion of the very expensive metal mouthpieces now on the market are expressly designed for this kind of playing.

An even greater variety of amplification devices is also now employed by saxophonists working in the pop field, but it is significant to note that the most successful are those who have given much thought and experimentation time to the best use of microphones. A good example is Lenny Pickett, who tries to preserve as much as possible of the true saxophone sound while balancing with the electric instruments.

The pop style of solo makes much use of the altissimo register, and conscientious players who practice this in a regular, systematic way, can develop a really fluent and very extended range, as the wide lay pop mouthpiece lends itself very readily to the production of harmonics.

Apart from this, the most interesting aspect to have arisen from pop style saxophone playing is the further confirmation of the saxophone's ability to mirror the human voice. In the past it has always been the instrument's flexibility and vocal qualities which have led to its effective use in such a wide variety of musical styles. This was the most obvious reason for it becoming such an important voice in jazz.

The thoughtful pop saxophonist should study the vocal inflexions of the lead singer, and mirror them in his playing. In this context it is informative to listen to the work of Curtis Stigers, a pop singer who performs with a saxophone slung around his neck instead of the usual guitar! When he takes a sax solo it's his own vocal he's answering and commenting upon. Not a situation that could ever arise in straight music, and interesting for that reason. Also, a pop star singer playing the saxophone must raise the profile of the instrument in the mind of the general public, which is a good thing for all of us, whether involved in the pop industry or not.

The Vintage Saxophone Revival

An interesting phenomenon of today's saxophone scene is the increasing demand for classic models of the pre-war era, particularly Selmers, Conns and Bueschers. Saxophone magazines abound with advertisements offering them for sale and searching for some particular model.

What is their attraction? It must lie in their tone; they seem to have a more centred sound than modern instruments, and, if they are in good condition, the low notes speak more easily. In many cases the bore is somewhat smaller than the instruments of today, which can seem tonally brash and overbearing in comparison.

It is no use playing a vintage saxophone with a modern mouthpiece; if you find one still with the original mouthpiece, that's fine, but it rarely happens. You have to search for the authentic round chamber mouthpieces to discover what such an instrument is intended to sound like.

The following list of Selmer serial numbers, which has just come into my hands by courtesy of Dave Aarons, via John Sands, has told me two things about my own best vintage saxophones. They are both 'cigar cutters'; I always knew this was a nickname referring to the unusually shaped piece of linkage on the automatic octave mechanism which has a hole in it like the device used in those days to chop the end off a cigar, but I have to confess that I never even knew the official name of the model, which I see now was 'Super Sax'; they have always been universally known as 'cigar cutters'.

My alto, (which was discovered by Fred Summerbell), belonged to the late Jack Wetherall, who did the saxophone work with the London Philharmonic Orchestra for many years, up to the 1960's. Its number is 15856, which dates it as a 1932 model. The mouthpiece I use with it is a Selmer Standard, which

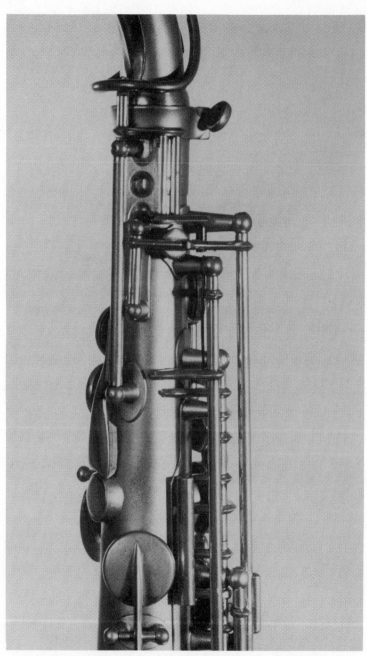

Close-up of the automatic octave mechanism on the Selmer 1930–33
Super Sax model, which gave it the nickname 'Cigar Cutter'

Close-up of the bell of a 1932 'Cigar Cutter' (author's collection)

is probably even older, as these mouthpieces were being made in the early 1920's. They are distinguished by a metal ring around the shank, and have a large round chamber similar to the Adolphe Sax original. Mine is marked 'Table B'.

My 'cigar-cutter' tenor is number 17578, so although a year younger than the alto, 1933, had not been nearly so well looked after.

Its origin is unknown until an ex-pupil of mine, Nigel Hinson, discovered it in Nottingham in a dreadful state of neglect. My instrument technician, Peter Snowdon, of Weybridge, Surrey, performed a miraculous resurrection job on it, and I now class it as the best saxophone I own. On it I use a Buescher mouthpiece, marked 'The Buescher, Elkhart, Indiana, U.S.A.' It has a thick collar around the shank, like the straight mouthpiece illustrated in Chapter 4.

If the current fashion for 'authentic' performance of music on original instruments spreads to the saxophone, then these vintage saxophones will be in even greater demand. A well known bass clarinet player was recently asking around the profession if anybody had a playable 'turn of the century' bass clarinet which he could use to perform 'authentic' Elgar.

So a similar demand for authentic saxophones is not out of the question, as many of the best known orchestral parts one performs were written during the 20's and 30's. Perhaps one day the manufacturers will be producing reproduction 'cigar cutters' for the authentic performance market. It would certainly be a step in the right direction if somebody would start making reproduction vintage round chamber mouthpieces!

Selmer Serial Numbers: 1922–1988

Model	*Year Manufacturered*	*Serial Numbers*
Model 22	1922	750-1400
Model 22	1923	1401-2350
Model 22	1924	2351-3350
Model 22	1925	3351-4450
Model 26	1926	4451-5600
Model 26	1927	5601-7850
Model 26	1928	7851-9700
Model 26	1929	9701-11950
Cigar Cutter/Super Sax	1930	11951-14000
Cigar Cutter/Super Sax	1931	14001-15750
Cigar Cutter/Super Sax	1932	15751-17250
Cigar Cutter/Super Sax	1933	17251-18700
Radio Improved	1934	18701-20100
Radio Improved	1935	20101-21750
Balanced Action	1936	21751-22650
Balanced Action	1937	22651-25600
Balanced Action	1938	25601-27650
Balanced Action	1939	27651-29300
Balanced Action	1940	29301-29750
Balanced Action	1941	29751-30500
Balanced Action	1942	30501-31150
Balanced Action	1943	31151-31580
Balanced Action	1944	31581-31850
Balanced Action	1945	31851-32350
Balanced Action	1946	32351-33700
Balanced Action	1947	33701-35800
Super Action	1948	35801-38500
Super Action	1949	38501-41500
Super Action	1950	41501-45100
Super Action	1951	45101-48300
Super Action	1952	48301-51800
Super Action	1953	51801-55200
Mark VI	1954	55201-59000
Mark VI	1955	59001-63400

Mark VI	1956	63401-68900
Mark VI	1957	68901-74500
Mark VI	1958	74501-80400
Mark VI	1959	80401-85200
Mark VI	1960	85201-91300
Mark VI	1961	91301-97300
Mark VI	1962	97301-104500
Mark VI	1963	104501-112500
Mark VI	1964	112501-121600
Mark VI	1965	121601-131800
Mark VI	1966	131801-141500
Mark VI	1967	141501-152400
Mark VI	1968	152401-162500
Mark VI	1969	162501-173800
Mark VI	1970	173801-184900
Mark VI	1971	184901-196000
Mark VI	1972	196001-208700
Mark VI	1973	208701-220800
Mark VII	1974	220801-233900
Mark VII	1975	233901-246800
Mark VII	1976	246801-261100
Mark VII	1977	261101-276100
Mark VII	1978	276101-289700
Mark VII	1979	289701-303100
Mark VII	1980	303101-315500
Super Action 80	1981	315501-327300
Super Action 80	1982	327301-340200
Super Action 80	1983	340201-353300
Super Action 80	1984	343301-366400
Super Action 80	1985	366401-378800
Super Action 80 Series II	1986	378801-391000
Super Action 80 Series II	1987	391001-406000
Super Action 80 Series II	1988	406001-

Buescher, Buffet, Conn and King Serial numbers and dates

Buescher

Serial No.	Year	Serial No.	Year
5000	1905	9669	1963
11250	1910	10064	1964
25103	1915	11749	1965
61255	1920	12778	1966
175275	1925	13766	1967
255250	1930	14487	1968
269000	1935	15347	1969
291000	1940	16323	1970
303000	1945	17319	1971
332000	1950	18445	1972
350000	1955	19787	1973
360000	1960	21441	1974
381000	1963	22687	1975
Bought out by Selmer		24417	1976
408818	1965	26151	1977
520000	1970	27280	1978
630000	1975	28733	1979
785000	1980	30190	1980
875000	1983	31539	1981
		32961	1982

Buffet

Serial No.	Year	Serial No.	Year
		33924	1983
2925	1952	34664	1984
3115	1953	35733	1985
3390	1954		
3763	1955	**Conn**	
4226	1956	9600	1905
4817	1957	10800	1906
5392	1958	12000	1907
6172	1959	13000	1908
6808	1960	15400	1909
7416	1961	17800	1910
8656	1962	21200	1911

Serial No.	Year	Serial No.	Year
22500	1912	327150	1948
25000	1913	332150	1949
30000	1914	337250	1950
35000	1916	341850	1951
40000	1917	341851	1952
50000	1919	354742	1953
58000	1920	359251	1954
64000	1921	500001	1955
83000	1922	571750	1956
101775	1923	652002	1957
124600	1924	718626	1958
145400	1925	779657	1959
167900	1926	834200	1960
193450	1927	898556	1961
209250	1928	949465	1962
224600	1929	C00501	1963
237800	1930	C73854	1964
244700	1931	E54106	1965
249230	1932	H31247	1966
256501	1933	K35274	1967
260000	1934		
263500	1935		
271000	1936	**King**	
278000	1937	5000	1915
284000	1938	78000	1925
285000	1939	126000	1930
288300	1940	161000	1935
295250	1941	220000	1940
304500	1942	275000	1945
309250	1943	305000	1950
309300	1944	340000	1955
310200	1945	370000	1960
314000	1946	406500	1965
320000	1947	457600	1970
		511750	1975

The World Saxophone Congress

Just as the saxophone was the invention of one man, so the WSC
was originally conceived by Paul Brodie, of Toronto. He first
mooted the idea at the Sherman House Hotel in Chicago, while
attending the 1968 Mid-West Band and Orchestra Clinic. With
the help of Eugene Rousseau the first WSC was organised to
take place as part of the 1969 Mid-West Band and Orchestra
Clinic.

Five hundred participants attended the event, including Cecil
Leeson, Marcel Mule, Sigurd Rascher and Larry Teal, who all
received Honorary Awards in recognition of their pioneering
work on behalf of the saxophone.

At first it was decided to hold a WSC every two years, but as
the numbers attending and the complexity of organisation
increased, the interval was extended to three years. The overall
planning of the WSC now comes under the auspices of The
North American Saxophone Alliance which publishes a maga-
zine/newsletter 'The Saxophone Symposium' four times a year.

Here is a list of the twelve WSC's which have so far taken place:

	Year	Venue	Principal Organiser(s)
1	1969	Chicago, USA	Paul Brodie/Eugene Rousseau
2	1970	Chicago	Donald Sinta/Paul Brodie
3	1972	Toronto, Canada	Paul Brodie/James Houlik
4	1974	Bordeaux, France	Jean-Marie Londeix
5	1976	The Royal College of Music London	Christopher Gradwell and the London Saxophone Quartet
6	1979	Northwestern University Evanston, Illinois, USA	Frederick Hemke/Eugene Rousseau
7	1982	Nuremberg, Germany	Gunter Priesner
8	1985	Washington, DC, USA	Steven Mauk, Reginald Jackson, Dale Underwood
9	1988	Tokyo, Japan	Yuichi Omuro
10	1992	Pesaro, Italy	Massimo Mazzoni
11	1997	Valencia, Spain	Juan Antonio Ramirez
12	2000	Montreal, Canada	Francois Guy & Noel Samyn

An historic event at the 1976 World Saxophone Congress.
Marcel Josse, who was a member of Marcel Mule's Quartet from 1936 to
1966, in a discussion group with Stephen Trier (L) and Marcel Mule (R)

The Clarinet And Saxophone Society Of Great Britain

This Society, usually called by its acronym 'CASS', was formed
in 1976, being partly inspired by the World Saxophone Congress
of that year, the first time such an important international
gathering of woodwind players had been held in Britain.

The prime mover in the formation of CASS was Alan Lucas,
at that time Managing Director of Buffet-Crampon UK Limited.
He arranged a meeting at the Russell Hotel, where he put the
idea to a number of active clarinet and saxophone players and
teachers. They agreed enthusiastically to recruit members,
arrange concerts and courses and to help with the production of
a quarterly magazine; so CASS was born.

From those small beginnings in a smoke-filled room on the
first floor of the Russell Hotel, CASS has grown to be an

internationally recognised society of over 1,000 members spread over 30 countries. A cross-section of its membership would reveal teachers, students, amateur and professional players, manufacturers and composers, all of whom have an interest in the instruments and their repertoire.

The quarterly magazine, *Clarinet and Saxophone* has steadily improved in quality of content and production until it now ranks as one of the leading magazines for woodwind players in the world. Much of the credit for this improvement must be given to Laurence of Mar, who recently retired after several years as editor.

The Society holds a summer conference each year, where in addition to concerts by leading artists and ensembles, there are opportunities for members to play in groups, participate in masterclasses and receive specialised coaching. In addition, there is an annual Spring teachers' course which covers all aspects of single reed teaching and smaller regional events are organised from time to time. The main conferences are held in a different part of the country each year; recent events have taken place in London, Manchester, Canterbury, Wakefield and Warwick.

CASS also regularly links up with like-minded organisations to put on other events. Several events have been held in conjunction with BASBWE (The British Association of Symphonic Bands and Wind Ensembles) and CASS had a substantial involvement in the 1993 ICA (International Clarinet Association) Clarfest in Ghent, Belgium, in which a whole day of the Festival was devoted to British players and music.

An important CASS development was the foundation in 1990 of the British Saxophone Congress, a biennial event which attracts many of the nation's top saxophone soloists and ensembles for a weekend of recitals, lectures, masterclasses and exhibitions. In addition, a guest artist is invited from abroad with Jean Yves Formeau taking part in 1990 and Eugene Rousseau in 1992.

At the time of writing the Membership Secretary of CASS is: Susan Moss, 167 Ellerton Road, Tolworth, Surrey KT6 7UB.

Epilogue

I've been writing this book in the year 1993, one year before the centenary of Adolphe Sax's death. I'd like to think of it as a kind of progress report for him on how his brainchild has been doing over the last century. So what can I tell him about the saxophone's current status that might really excite him?

Well, for one thing, even as I write, a saxophone player is being inaugurated as the President of the United States of America. That now makes two world Heads of State who play the saxophone. King Bhumibol of Thailand has been a well known saxophone enthusiast for many years, and he is now joined by Mr Bill Clinton.

King Bhumibol Adulyadej was born in Cambridge, Massachusetts, while his father was studying at Harvard Medical School. In later years he led his own Dixieland band while studying in Switzerland.

In 1976, when I was involved with the organisation of the World Saxophone Congress in London, I wrote to the King of Thailand inviting him to open the Congress (well, it was worth a try, I thought).

I received a nice reply from an aide, saying that His Majesty would be detained in Bangkok by affairs of state at that time, but was most interested to hear of the WSC and wished us every success with the event. So we had to make do with Marcel Mule instead to open to Congress, but he's King of the saxophonists anyway!

The milestone in saxophone history, which I think would please Adolphe Sax the most, occurred in 1984. That was when the saxophone became the first musical instrument to be played in space! Yes, I do mean outer space, beyond the earth's atmosphere.

The five man crew of the February 1984 Challenger space shuttle included a physicist, Dr Ronald E McNair, who was an enthusiastic amateur tenor saxophone player. He conceived the idea of taking a saxophone on a space flight the year before, when he first knew that he might be chosen as a crew member, but a tenor was out of the question because of its size. It would have to be a soprano, he decided, but then discovered that a straight soprano is an inch and a half too long for an astronaut's personal storage compartment on a space shuttle!

So that is why it came about that the first musical instrument to be played in outer space was a CURVED SOPRANO SAXOPHONE! I find this extremely ironic from a personal point of view, because, during all the years I've been writing about the saxophone in various magazines, readers and editors have always seemed eager to drag me into the straight versus curved soprano controversy.

Although I personally prefer the straight-bodied soprano I have always conscientiously listed the advantages of the curved soprano, but I never thought to mention that it would be easier to stow on a spacecraft!

Ron McNair took the problems of playing in weightless and low pressure conditions very seriously. He wanted to be able to play the instrument well, because of the possibility that it might be heard on a broadcast from space. To help him in this respect he approached a California saxophone teacher, Kurt Heisig.

Drawing on experience gained in playing at high altitude in the mountains, Mr Heisig was able to advise on choice of reeds and preparatory exercises for playing in the low air pressure of the spacecraft cabin.

What neither of them was able to predict were the effects of zero gravity. When Ron finally had a chance to get his saxophone out of its plastic wrapping and play it in space, he found the biggest problem to be the moisture in the instrument. Normally this runs 'down' the bore, but in space there is no 'down'. The water succumbed to molecular attraction and formed water balls which collected in all the tone holes. Also the pads were not sealing well in the extremely dry, filtered air of the shuttle.

But he certainly did play his saxophone out there in space, although, for some unknown reason, it was not broadcast for the world to hear. He did make a tape, but, unfortunately, it was accidentally erased in the course of all the electronic business which goes on in a space shuttle.

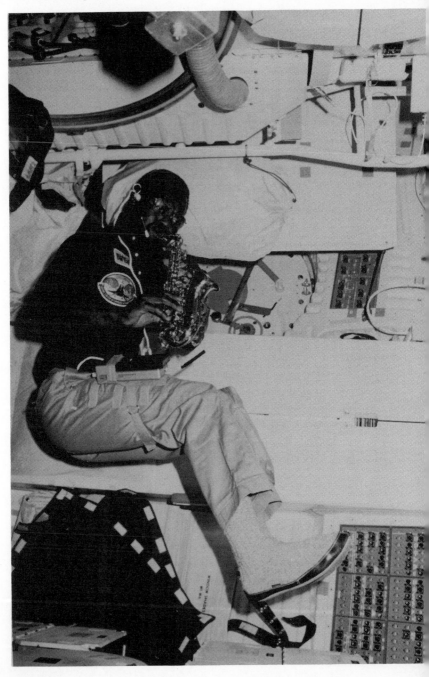

Ron McNair was selected for another space shuttle mission, and he had great hopes of taking his saxophone again and, this time, getting it broadcast. He did indeed launch with the next shuttle, but it was the tragic launch of January 28th 1986, when the space shuttle blew up and everyone on board was killed. Some sources maintain that he had his saxophone with him, others say that it was not aboard.

Be that as it may, the fact remains that, in 1984, Dr Ronald E McNair, NASA astronaut, was the first person to play a musical instrument in outer space, and that instrument was a SAXOPHONE.

Opposite page

THE FIRST MUSICAL INSTRUMENT TO BE PLAYED IN SPACE

8th February 1984. Dr. Ronald E. McNair playing the soprano saxophone in a weightless condition aboard the Space Shuttle Challenger
Note the words 'Window Shades' on the right of the picture, which indicate the real direction of 'up' and 'down'
(Photo by courtesy of NASA, Houston, Texas)

Eighteen
The Bottom Line

As I've been writing this book I've shown sections of it to many of my pupils, both young and adult, and discussed with other teachers and colleagues in the profession what to include. The sum of their reactions impels me to add this postscript, which is in the nature of an exhortation to young players (and a reminder to their teachers) not to lose sight of the basic essentials of musical saxophone playing in a mass of interesting but inessential trivia.

What I mean is this; the young players all wanted to know things like fingerings for altissimo notes and how to do circular breathing; in the vast majority of cases trying to run before they can walk! Many adults were mainly interested in the obsolete instruments of the 1920's or looked for information on their favourite jazz idol.

Yes, all these things are fascinating, and should, of course, be in a book about the saxophone, but they are not essential for the well equipped player, so I feel it is my duty to underline the qualities which it should be your priority to develop. These are the things which various categories of people with whom you will interact as a player will be looking for. As you go through life as a musician you are continually being assessed by a variety of people (other than audiences, who are comparatively easy to please) and either passing muster or being found wanting. The people I have in mind are: examiners, adjudicators, conductors, fixers and orchestral managers, bandleaders, composers, critics, record producers, sound balancers and, worst of all, other players, especially of other instruments!

There is no doubt what your principal preoccupation now and

for the rest of your life has to be; it's the 'BIG I'; INTONATION! No matter how brilliant your technique, how exquisite your sound, if you play out of tune all your other efforts will have been wasted. Other players will hate and despise you. In orchestras the bald headed viola player with the red neck and big ears (there's one in every orchestra) will look round with a horrified expression, and in big band sax sections there will be remarks such as 'We're showing more cork this year, man!'

The best advice I can give you is to listen to every note you play. Getting the mouthpiece in the right place for the tuning note, be it A or B♭, is only a start. The saxophone is a victim of its own flexibility and you must approach it as if you are singing, pitching each note with your throat, oral cavity and air support.

It's particularly difficult to play in tune with a piano, yet much of your most important playing; exams, competitions, auditions and recitals will be with piano accompaniment. A good intonation exercise is to sit at the piano with your saxophone slung round your neck. Put your right foot on the sustaining pedal, play a note on the piano, then play the same note on the saxophone, with a completely straight sound; no vibrato. Continue this until you've tried all the notes on the saxophone. This is not to say that all pianos are perfectly in tune, far from it, but it's you who has to adjust; the piano isn't going to!

The next most important thing to cultivate is TONE, and you must have the flexibility either to sing out a big solo or to produce a sound which will blend with other instruments. The lack of this quality is most often evident in Wind Bands, conductors of which often complain that their saxophone section sticks out like a sore thumb. The horns are sometimes referred to as the bridge between woodwind and brass, so the saxophones should be the bridge between woodwind and horns. If you're on alto listen to the flutes and oboes when you're playing high and to the horns as you go lower. If you're on tenor listen to the horns when high and to the bassoons when low.

The fact that many of the great jazz players developed an instantly recognisable tone is one of the most significant aspects of the 20th century development of the saxophone. However, this can lead to dangerous paths for young players. If you imitate

141

your favourite jazz legend, then you will be put down as a clone of whoever it is. If you develop your own individual sound, that can be dangerous unless you yourself are a jazz great. If you're not, then you won't be able to make a living just playing jazz with your own group, and you'll have to do all kinds of other jobs on which your individual sound may not be appropriate. Flexibility, adaptability and versatility are the most important attributes of the successful working saxophonist, and the ability to produce a controlled vibrato of any speed and width or a perfectly straight sound if required, will be your greatest tonal asset.

The third essential is ACCURATE SIGHT READING, which applies, of course, to all instruments. I'm not referring to great musical interpretation, which comes later with more practice and rehearsal, but just to the basic requirement of playing the right notes in the right place with the right rhythm and the phrasing which is written.

I do so much teaching that I'm an expert on what people do wrong, believe me! In the case of notes . . . well, suffice it to say that I keep a stuffed parrot perched in my teaching room, holding a notice in its beak saying, 'Accidentals stay through the bar!' As for rhythm, the favourite thing is rushing; whenever a group of semiquavers appears they are often played too fast. If the semiquavers go on longer, however, they will probably get slower, and the tempo increases again when the music gets easier. As regards phrasing, some people like to tongue everything, while others want to slur everything. I've never worked out why they divide initially into these two preferential groups. It's much easier to play the phrasing as written, and, in the case of big band playing, it's one of the most essential ingredients of a good sax section.

Lastly, a problem which is peculiar to the saxophone, owing to its very conical bore; you must be able to play LOW NOTES SOFTLY. The worst situation is when you go to play in an orchestra.

As soon as you open the lid of the case the conductor will be putting his finger to his lips! So many of the big orchestral saxophone solos have soft passages below bottom D, and that bald headed, red necked, big eared viola player will be turning round with a sneer if you can't control them!

But it's not only a problem in symphony orchestras; it often arises in shows, especially when you're playing under a singer, and in quartet playing it's extremely important. The essential aids are: all pads covering well, strong springs on closed-standing keys, a mouthpiece with a sensible lay, not too hard a reed, firm finger pressure, plenty of air support and . . . practice!

So, to sum up, the essential subjects which should be your priority considerations are: intonation, tone, accurate sight reading and soft low notes. If you are always thinking about those four areas everything else will look after itself; technique is just a matter of practising scales and arpeggios as much as possible. By all means enjoy looking into the less essential but fascinating aspects of saxophone playing and history, but never lose sight of the BIG FOUR BASICS!

Index